ROSSVILLE FLATS

The Rise and Fall

Compiled by Jim Collins

GUILDHALL PRESS

To all the residents of the Rossville Flats, 1966–1989

First published June 2019.

Copyright © Guildhall Press/Jim Collins.

Images © Jim Collins, Terry Lamberton, Moloney Collection, The Willie Carson Collection, Heritage Ireland, *Derry Journal*, Eamon Melaugh, Phil Cunningham, Frankie McMenamin, Lee McDaid, Joseph Keys, Seamus Breslin, Jordan Sheaffer, Ivan Hetherington, Colin Palin, Ivan Ballard, Michael Burns, Gilles Peress, Fulvio Grimaldi, Museum of Free Derry and various contributors.

Guildhall Press
Ráth Mór Centre
Bligh's Lane
Derry BT48 0LZ
T: (028) 7136 4413
www.ghpress.com

Layout/design by Joe McAllister
Hive Studios
www.hivestudio.org
T: (028) 7127 7487

Cover design by Denise Meenan and Joe McAllister.

Supported by the Housing Executive.

A CIP catalogue record for this book is available from the British Library.

ISBN 978 1 911053 40 8

Acknowledgements

Many thanks to all those who participated in the original oral history project and/or contributed to the production of this publication. These include: Peter McCartney, Eddie Breslin, Frankie McMenamin, Charlie McMenamin, Seamus Keenan, Annette Harkin, Billy Carlin, Celine Carlin, Don Carlin, Deirdre Conaghan, Eileen Collins, Kieran Pritchard, Martin Dunleavy, Dr Máirtín Ó Catháin, Robert Green, John Tierney, Philomena Wilson, Sheila Brown, Tommy McCourt, Stephen Ryan, Gareth Cross, Siobhan Mallon, Marta Mhic Giolla Aolain, PRONI, *Derry Journal* and *Derry News*.

Our gratitude to all those who provided images: Jim Collins, Terry Lamberton, Lee McDaid, Joseph Keys, Seamus Breslin, Jordan Sheaffer, John Nelis, Ivan Hetherington, Colin Palin, Ivan Ballard, Seamus McCloskey, Phil Cunningham, Hugh Gallagher, Eamon Melaugh, Michael Burns, Gilles Peress, Fulvio Grimaldi, Museum of Free Derry, Camerawork, *Derry Journal*, Heritage Ireland, Gasyard Heritage Centre, The Willie Carson Collection and Moloney Collection. Apologies to anyone if we have unwittingly included your image without acknowledgement from any source.

A special thanks to everyone who contributed a wealth of information and images to the Rossville Flats Facebook page that greatly enhanced the project.

We are grateful to the Housing Executive for their financial support which made this publication possible.

Our appreciation to the following sources referenced:
Brian Barton, 'Relations between Westminster and Stormont during the Attlee premiership', in *Irish Political Studies* (1992).
CEB Brett, *Housing a Divided Community* (Institute of Public Administration, Dublin, 1986).
Mickey Cooper, *From Columba to Conflict* (Gasyard Development Trust, 2012).
Phil Cunningham, *Reflections of Derry* (Guildhall Press, 2004).
Edward Daly, *Mister, Are You a Priest?* (Four Courts Press, Dublin, 2000).
Willie Deery, *Springtown Camp: from the inside* (Guildhall Press, 2010).
Miles Glendinning, Stefan Muthesius, *Tower Block: Modern Public Housing in England, Scotland, Wales and Northern Ireland* (Yale University Press, New Haven, CT, 1994).
John Lindsay, *Brits Speak Out* (Guildhall Press, 1998).
Eamon Melaugh, *Derry's Troubled Years* (Guildhall Press, 2018).
Sinéad Power, 'The development of the Ballymun housing scheme, Dublin, 1965-1969', in *Irish Geography* (2000).
Brendan Mc Keever, *If Streets Could Speak* (Guildhall Press, 2018).

Foreword

The Rossville Flats are an iconic landmark in the historical and political landscape of the north of Ireland. They were born out of the necessities of ward manipulation by the Londonderry Corporation and an obsessive contemporary trend by town planners throughout Ireland and Britain to ease housing pressure by building cheap high-rise complexes.

The first negative impact of the Rossville Flats was the disruption of the local community. Whole streets were bulldozed to make way for their development, mainly the Lecky Road and Rossville Street. This was carried out in flagrant disregard for 97 per cent of the residents and business people of the area who had expressed their opposition to the plans in a survey. The next impact of the flats was – as a direct result of their bleak vistas, lack of facilities, substandard materials and poorly resourced maintenance – a growing alienation of the hundreds of families, many with young children, who called them home. Despite assurances as to their modernity and convenience, they were in reality a vertical ghetto.

However, in the context of the civil rights movement in the late 1960s and the accompanying sense of common purpose, this alienation turned into solidarity. The flat dwellers began to agitate against the conditions in the flats: the flooding and damp, the fires, the rats, the noise, the lack of privacy, minimal children's play areas, and the lifts that didn't work. British soldiers soon occupied the roof causing local youth to daub HM Prison Rossville on the wall beside the main entrance.

This publication emerged from a wider project to record a social/oral history of the flats and their residents. The story of the flats is the story of the people who lived in them and how they coped with, and then struggled against, the increasingly unacceptable conditions. Eventually their solidarity and perseverance in the face of obstinate officialdom won through and they witnessed the destruction between 1986–1989 of the concrete monolith so grandiosely erected 23 years earlier. Paradoxically, in spite of widespread relief at their demolition, many of the flat dwellers look back with nostalgia at the times they spent there. As one resident put it: 'If they were there today I'd still be there, providing I still had my old neighbours.'

In the project interviews conducted, however, many young mothers in particular remarked they were in no hurry to go back to struggling with prams up urine-soaked stairs or worrying about letting children out to play with no adequate facilities.

This published account presents for outsiders a unique opportunity to discover the real-life experiences and testimonies of ordinary people who lived in the flats. As such, it is likely for many to be an eye-opener. It may well also provide the basis for real and meaningful discussion between communities, especially around the crucial issues of homelessness and the absence of state provision for affordable social housing.

With some 50 years since the establishment of the Derry Housing Action Committee, it is essential we learn the lessons of the past. Today we face an even more critical housing problem. It is time we recalled the spirit of these community initiatives and particularly the long battle fought by Rossville Flats' residents who ultimately won, due to their determination and resilience, the basic human right to a decent roof over their head.

Jim Collins
Community artist and former resident

Contents

Contributors

The following is a selection of former residents of the Rossville Flats and others who contributed to this publication and the oral/social history project carried out several years ago by Jim Collins, Terry Lamberton, Eddie Breslin, Charlie and Frankie McMenamin and associates. Extracts from their interviews, along with additional material from a variety of other sources, have been used to illustrate what life was like for those living in, or associated with, the flats over the 23 years of their existence.

Eddie Breslin was assistant caretaker in the Rossville Flats from 1978 to 1986 and has worked with the Housing Executive for nearly 40 years.

Sheila (Susan) Brown moved from Greenwalk in Creggan to 30 Mura Place in the Rossville Flats with her family of six in 1966. Sheila's daughter Rosemary, widely known as Dana, was resident in the flats when she won the Eurovision Song Contest as an 18-year-old in 1970.

Billy Carlin left Creggan with his parents and brother in 1973 and settled into 8 Donagh Place on the top floor of the Rossville Flats where he lived until 1980.

Don and **Celine Carlin** took up residence in a one-bedroom flat at 30 Donagh Place in 1966 when they moved from a small apartment beside the Rocking Chair bar in Waterloo Street.

Eileen Collins moved from Union Street in the Bogside into her two-bedroom flat at 20 Garvan Place in 1967 with her young son, Jim. Eileen was involved in the ongoing protests after British soldiers occupied the roof.

Deirdre Conaghan moved to 22 Garvan Place in the flats as a 17-year-old with her family in 1981 and later raised her own two children there. Her 'claim to fame' is that she was the last person to move out of the Rossville Flats in 1988.

Martin Dunleavy was only a month old when his family moved into 5 Garvan Place in May 1966. He went on to become a caretaker in the flats working alongside his father John who was also a caretaker.

Annette Harkin was born in the flats in 1972, just under three weeks after Bloody Sunday. She spent the first eleven years of her life at 48 Donagh Place in a family of nine.

Seamus Keenan is a Derry playwright, poet and author who won the Hennessey New Irish Writer Award in 2003. His acclaimed work includes the BBC short film *Do Armed Robbers Have Love Affairs?* and his 2014 play *Over The Wire.*

Terry Lamberton moved from Nailor's Row into 47 Donagh Place with his older brother and parents in 1967, one week after his first birthday. They eventually left the flats in 1981.

Martha McClelland (Marta Mhic Giolla Aolain), originally from North America, moved into 25 Mura Place in 1981, just above the row of shops in block two of the Rossville Flats where she stayed for several years.

Thomas McCourt was a member of the Young Socialists and helped set up Radio Free Derry when the Battle of the Bogside erupted in the shadow of the flats in August 1969.

Frankie and **Charlie McMenamin** had nothing but happy memories of their time spent in the Rossville Flats with their grandparents, the Caseys, who moved from Nelson Street into 67 Mura Place in 1967.

Maureen Morrison moved from two attic rooms in the Bogside to 38 Mura Place in 1966 with her husband Joe and two young children.

Dr Máirtín Ó Catháin is Senior Lecturer in Modern Irish History at the School of Humanities and Social Sciences at the University of Central Lancashire, Preston. He is the postgraduate course lead and history moderation and externals lead.

John Tierney was a local councillor, mayor of Derry and MLA. He lived at 12 Donagh Place for several years and was instrumental in the campaign to have the flats demolished.

Philomena (Philly) Wilson moved with her husband and their four children from St Columb's Wells to Donagh Place in the Rossville Flats in 1970 before relocating to William Street several years later.

Rossville Flats – An Overview

The Rossville Flats were built by the John Laing group under contract from the Londonderry Corporation and Northern Ireland Housing Trust as part of the Rossville Street/Lecky Road redevelopment scheme. The sectra-system, concrete-based, interlinked high-rise complex with covered access walkways was originally designed to house 178 families. First occupied in 1966, the multi-storey flats had floor sections designated as Garvan Place, Mura Place and Donagh Place.

The Northern Ireland Housing Executive (NIHE) was established in 1971 as the result of the reform of housing administration and local government. All housing stock held by local government and development agencies was transferred to the NIHE. The new body recruited its own architects, engineers and quantity surveyors as well as housing and administrative staff totalling 2,800 employees by 1973. The NIHE carried out various improvements and refurbishments on the Rossville Flats over the years including adding the primary-coloured doors and panels between windows in the early 1980s. As a result, the complex was often referred to locally as 'Derry's Rubik's Cube'.

The flats gained global recognition during the Troubles, being the scene of some of the worst rioting from the Battle of the Bogside in 1969 onwards and the focal point of Bloody Sunday in 1972. After a sustained campaign by the residents of the flats for their demolition because of the deteriorating living conditions, the NI Office and Housing Executive finally acquiesced. Block one was demolished in 1986 and the remaining two housing blocks were knocked down in 1989.

HM Prison Rossville

By Seamus Keenan

Near the site of the country market in Derry's old Bogside – where cows and pigs, goats and donkeys, day-old chicks and scrawny boilers, horses, sheep and the occasional embarrassed goldfish were bought and sold – the city planners built the Rossville Flats. And the people loved them. They were habitable, modern, sophisticated. We no longer had country hicks, but city slickers, with our very own version of a New York skyline. At night, Bogsiders would trek to Creggan to look down on the eighth wonder of the world and all its twinkling glory.

In the 1960s, high-rise accommodation seemed like the future. It dealt effectively and cheaply with the lack of housing space, and in local terms, it enabled the ruling Unionist Corporation, conveniently, to maintain their old gerrymandering system. The flats were a landmark, a colourful contrast to the rows of tiny terraced housing and their outdoor toilets and polished doorsteps. Someone once described high rises as 'Vertical Communities', and there was much truth in that. Hundreds of families, with their children, and their cats, and their grannies and grandas, moved in. A little row of shops sprang up. At one time or another, most of Derry must have staggered into the queue in the little hallway of the Chinese restaurant for their Saturday-night curries, a new cuisine for a new neighbourhood.

Then came 1969 and the Battle of the Bogside. The RUC were on the verge of overrunning the area when some military genius realised the strategic importance of the flats. A group of young men seized the roofs, gaining control of the entire Bogside. CS gas couldn't shift them, and they remained there until the British Government pulled the RUC out, replacing them with the British Army.

All through the 1970s and '80s the Rossville Flats were the flash point area in the ongoing war on our streets. Some of the men who lived in the flats, who had fought on its rooftops, died in its huge shadow on Bloody Sunday and in other tragic confrontations over the subsequent years. It had become a battleground, a haven, an outlandish place of misery and fun. The British Army set up lookout posts on top of it. And children were still being born and raised there. But years of political struggle had sharpened people's desire for justice in all its forms and as living conditions in the flats deteriorated, the levels of dissent soared.

Water poured down the bathroom walls, the homes were cold and draughty, and the patch-up renovations were all highly expensive and totally ineffective. The optimism of the early sixties was short-lived. By the mid-eighties, the inhabitants of the flats regularly described their home as HM Prison Rossville and the tenants' committees, with their local parties, fought a long campaign for their demolition. Eventually, by 1989, the Rossville Flats were tumbled and the place looked really strange. In fact, it looked like a place that could be used as an outdoor cattle market.

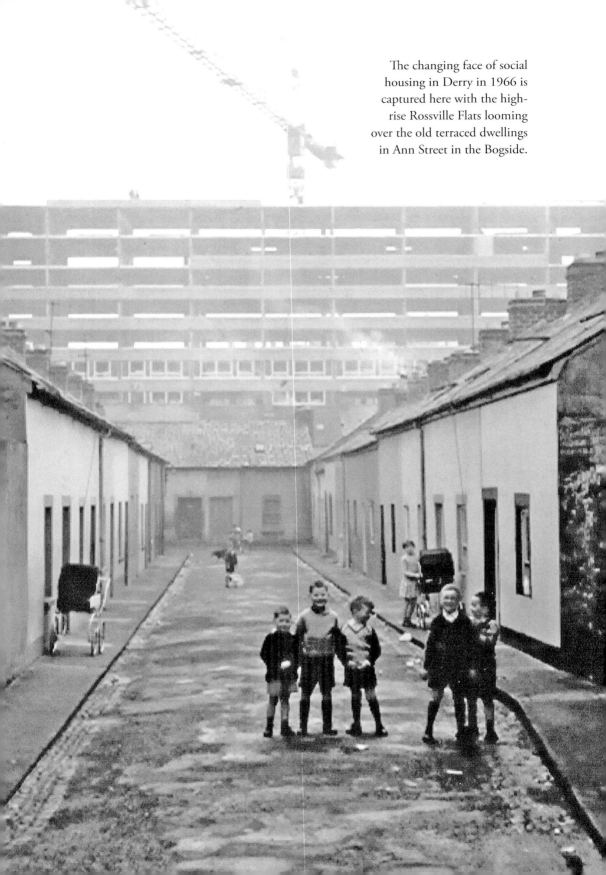

The changing face of social housing in Derry in 1966 is captured here with the high-rise Rossville Flats looming over the old terraced dwellings in Ann Street in the Bogside.

Derry's Skyscraper Flats
By Dr Máirtín Ó Catháin

The plan that led to the construction of the Rossville Flats grew out of a number of competing demands, interests and pressures. The two central facets were the creation of the Northern Ireland Housing Trust (NIHT) in 1945 by Stormont and the so-called 'slum clearance' project known as the Rossville Street/Lecky Road redevelopment scheme. Of course, directing all of this and determining where the flats would eventually be built was the sectarian nature of Derry's gerrymandered electoral boundaries.

In Derry, the housing situation was particularly acute with a wide array of sub-standard, small and completely inadequate nineteenth-century housing which had compelled people, particularly in the greater Bogside area, to seize and occupy abandoned army Nissen huts across the city. The Corporation evicted and prosecuted many of these brave families but were forced to concede the existence of Springtown Camp, where a decade and more later people were still living as redevelopment got under way in the Bogside.

Fahan Street and old Bogside in the early 1960s with the cattle market on the right.

The idea of a 'slum clearance' had been suggested in 1958 but it was probably only through a sit-in by a group of Springtown women at the Guildhall in 1959 that the Corporation were forced to look again at the housing issue in Derry. Public demands for reform and more and better housing were growing.

Finally, in 1960, the NIHT were given the task of redeveloping the Rossville Street/Lecky Road area with the same proviso which had applied to previous house building in Creggan – that all housing was to be concentrated in the South Ward. This was to protect the gerrymandered electoral ward boundaries which maintained Unionist power in the city.

It was an unholy alliance between the Trust's desire for what it believed was modern and architecturally imaginative high-rise housing and the Corporation's concern to retain population density in the same area that created the Rossville Flats. Other housing developments by the Trust, such as in Belfast, had managed 'slum clearance' through a mixture of 'de-canting' to suburban estates and high-rise blocks, such as at Cregagh and Divis. In Derry, however, and notwithstanding the wishes of residents to stay in the local area, the only way was up (literally), or so it seemed.

The NIHT Rossville Street/Lecky Road redevelopment scheme appeared in the *Derry Journal* complete with map on 21 February 1961, though the core of the plan had been circulating for a short time before this. A local business committee

Rossville Street in the early 1960s.

had already emerged saying the scheme threatened to put two-thirds of them out of business and vowing to oppose it; they clashed with local councillors at a meeting early in February in the West End Hall.

The Trust's General Manager, JG Calvert, promised that no children would be rehoused in the flats though this was later seen as impractical. Within a few days of the redevelopment scheme appearing resistance was beginning to crystallise and the business interests were joined by residents who arranged a canvas of local views in the Rossville Street/Lecky Road area before approaching the Corporation. The result was that local people, many of whom had relatives in high-rise flats in England and Scotland, were said to be 'heavily against this type of accommodation'. The spokespersons for the residents, Stephen McGonagle, James McKane, Margaret Morrison and Hugh Harkin, said they were not against the scheme in principle, just some of the detail and whilst they'd heard a lot from the Trust about its 'architectural showpiece', they felt the Corporation had moved too fast, too soon and in the wrong direction.

Months of debate and acrimony followed with businesses worried about receiving the level of compensation they expected and residents battling to have the flats replaced by more conventional housing. Some of the Nationalist Party councillors, chiefly but not solely James Doherty and Séamus Deeney, came out in support of the scheme which they saw as 'big and imaginative' whilst the voices of local Labour Party figures such as Stephen McGonagle and Séamus Quinn remained critical. The *Derry Journal* had earlier given a cautious welcome to the scheme and the Catholic Bishop of Derry, Neil Farren, later supported such a view and appealed for 'goodwill' all round during his Easter homily.

After a public inquiry in June 1961 it was finally announced that Stormont had accepted the plans in their entirety with the Town Clerk notifying the public that copies of the approved scheme would be made available. A subsequent model of the scheme clearly marked out the 'skyscraper flats' though the government declared only one block of flats would be built in the interim 'until it is seen how the tenants chosen react to this new mode of living'. Firm details of the project were not published, however, until December 1964.

The *Derry Journal* reproduced a fairly fanciful artist's impression of the 'skyscraper flats' and stated they would cover the two-acre site of the cattle market and be completed in just 15 months. It noted the contract consisted of two 10-storey blocks containing a total of 138 flats with what it called 18 'bedsitting room' flats, 22 one-bedroom flats, 70 two-bedroom flats, 10 three-bedroom flats, and 18 three-bedroom maisonettes. The report added that on the ground floor of the blocks there would be six shop units, 28 garages and tenants' stores. Open car parking for a further 52 vehicles was added to the much-vaunted perks of the new homes alongside central heating and 'panoramic windows … in all living rooms'.

The new, and supposedly very time-efficient, sectra building system employed by builders John Laing to erect the Rossville Flats was very similar to ones in Sunderland and Tower Hamlets in London as well as the Divis complex in Belfast. The speed of construction may have been responsible for some of the problems which soon manifested themselves in the flats, but other issues had an impact. Charles Brett, later chair of the Housing Executive, wrote of how:

'… the cold bridge effect in deck-access blocks, leading to severe condensation, has now been clearly diagnosed. The perils inherent in the use of various concrete-based non-traditional methods of construction have become widely realised. The consequences of poorly installed plastic plumbing systems are all too evident. The inadequacies of chute-based rubbish disposal systems are now apparent.'

The reality is that many of these problems actually emerged within a very short time and had been foreseen by many of the residents and campaigners against the flats, just as the use of flat, as opposed to pitched, roofs in Meenan Park and other parts of the area was clearly a poorly thought-out idea.

By early 1965, building was well under way on the cattle market site while elsewhere arguments over levels of compensation for businesses affected by the redevelopment rumbled on. Hugh Harley, who was secretary of a committee set up to put the case for the business community, claimed that some people had already been evicted without compensation. A case at the Recorder's Court the previous year for new pub licences highlighted how starkly the area was changing. During

the case, the City Solicitor, Mr AW Jack, stated that there were 27 public houses in the redevelopment area, meaning one pub per 188 of the population whereas the scheme envisaged reducing this to just eight pubs, one per 600 people.

The question of Housing Trust rents arose in May 1965 when the Trust chair addressed a meeting in St Mary's Hall, Creggan, called to protest against impending rent increases on 200 houses. Calvert, the NIHT General Manager, said that he felt it wasn't unreasonable to expect people who had possession of their homes for several years to bear some more contribution to the building of new houses in the redevelopment scheme. Nationalist Party leader Eddie McAteer called the meeting a fruitful one but appealed for better consultation in future while the Derry Labour Party leader Stephen McGonagle encouraged tenants to form groups and bring pressure on the Trust – he added that unit for unit, flats cost twice the price of traditional houses to build and warned that further rises might come. Calvert responded that there wasn't a great difference and therefore the building of the flats made no great change in total costs for the Trust.

On 10 May 1966, the *Derry Journal* revealed that the new Rossville Flats had finally received their first tenants – a show flat had been opened in February to allow people to view the properties. The paper reported that a total of 18 flats, a mixture of two- and four-bedroom units, had been allocated on the first floor of the now downsized nine-storey block on Rossville Street. It noted the first two families moved in over the weekend of 7–8 May and the rest would take possession later in the week.

One of the first to move in was Mr Archibald Henderson from Thomas Street with his wife and two baby girls. When the first floor of block one was fully occupied the remainder of the block would be allocated floor by floor as work to complete the second block on Joseph Street was nearing completion. By August, nearly all of the 60 flats and nine maisonettes had been completed though there were still eight or nine vacant flats on the upper floors. There was at this time some delay in finishing block two, but work had already begun on a third six-/seven-storey block facing Fahan Street agreed to by the Trust some time previously. The first two blocks comprised nine storeys and at 120 feet high they were the tallest buildings in the city and the tenants interviewed by the *Journal* seemed generally pleased though the lack of proper drying facilities was an issue.

The flats were divided into three horizontal sections, excluding the ground floors which contained garages, shops and storage areas. The first three floors of blocks one and two (along with the lowest floor of block three) were known as Garvan Place. The next three floors of the three blocks formed Mura Place and the top three floors formed Donagh Place.

At 9 Garvan Place, Mrs Mottram – who had moved in with her husband Vincent and two children from Abbey Street and whose parents also lived in the new flats – said she had trained her two-year-old to stay on the veranda and praised the caretaker,

David Patterson, for his work in looking after the block. He had moved from 19 Stanley's Walk and now lived in the block, commenting that most people seemed satisfied with the new housing. An 18-year-old girl, Patricia McGilloway living at 9 Donagh Place, told the paper, 'I think it is great. My parents really are dying about it.'

As 1967 dawned, the flats were finally completed and the tenants began adjusting to their new lives. The first two blocks had cost in the region of £500,000. The city's loan debt had risen £300,000 to almost £4 million and it was clear rate rises were on the horizon. New housing had provided homes for those made homeless by redevelopment but it did little or nothing to tackle the wider housing needs in

the city and housing would be key for a new activist generation of socialists and Republicans. Some of these conducted an early survey amongst the tenants of the flats in the summer of 1967 soon after tenants themselves had lodged their first protests with the Corporation over the conversion of the children's play area in the inner courtyard into a car park.

Of the 111 tenants surveyed (the flats contained about 180 families), 71 per cent said they would have preferred traditional-type houses. The average number of bedrooms in the flats was two and the average number of people per flat was

four with an average rent of £1-17-3½ compared with an average previous rent of £0-17-7½. Several issues were raised, including a need for something to be done about better soundproofing for the flats. This last issue was noted by the young parish priest who would later become bishop, Edward Daly. He regularly visited the flats to bless the house when a new family moved in and remembered how:

'Tenants were … obliged to live in very close proximity with other occupants and the dividing walls were thin … a small and insignificant family row could be heard in three or four adjacent units. There was little privacy. Shortly after the flats were opened, I was called one night to curb the enthusiasm of a budding Benny Goodman who chose to practise his clarinet at 2.00am. His musical gifts were not greatly appreciated by neighbours over a wide area.'

In July 1968, the Trust announced a rent increase of between three to six shillings a week and the first Rossville Flats tenants' association declared they would be taking what they called a 'very militant stand' against the increases. The association was chaired by Roy Harkin, 53 Mura Place, with assistant chair Willie Doherty of 8 Donagh Place. The secretary was Patrick Downey, 57 Donagh Place, and the joint treasurers were given as Mrs Sheila Brown, Mura Place, and Jim Morrison, 38 Mura Place.

The letters announcing the increase were passed by tenants to the association who claimed they were already subsidising other Trust properties through the higher rents. A meeting called soon after, at which Liam Kelly, the deputy leader of

Family and friends of Kevin O'Hagan celebrate his birthday in the high flats.

the Republican Labour Party in Belfast spoke, struck a defiant tone and added that proper playing facilities and soundproof walls remained an issue alongside poor finishing work in many of the flats.

The rent increases led to widespread community mobilisation throughout the summer of that year and co-ordinated activity by a range of tenants' associations in some cases inspired and challenged by one another as well as by the Derry Housing Action Committee which had emerged the previous year.

By the time of the 5 October 1968 civil rights march, the residents of the Rossville Flats had started out on a new and dramatic period of their lives. For many, the flats represented hope for the future and the possibility that things might just finally be changing for a generation of Bogsiders. But if there was optimism and belief in the utopian ideas of the planners there was also a recognition that it was only by fighting for their rights that these things might come to pass.

Ordinary working-class people had fought the redevelopment, the Trust and the Corporation to improve the quality of their lives and protect the town and environment they cared about. But a much bigger fight against the very state that tried to dictate the limits of their lives and aspirations was looming on the horizon. That fight would go far beyond the flats. But here, too, the people of Donagh, Garvan and Mura would stand up and defy the state and its diktats to create a better life for themselves and their children and grandchildren.

Taking Care of the Flats
By Eddie Breslin

Eddie Breslin was one of several caretakers at the Rossville Flats over their existence and has been with the Housing Executive for nearly 40 years. He shared his memories of the flats and the people he met there with Derry News *reporter Gareth Cross in 2017.*

I was assistant caretaker in the Rossville Flats from 1978 to 1986. My job was to maintain the flats, balconies and stairways, communal bins and car parks. I started off working with John Dunleavy who was the head caretaker at the time and he lived in the building. The original caretaker was Davy Patterson who was there when the flats opened in 1966. There were a few other assistants such as Martin Dunleavy (John's son), Paddy Miller, Lee Barlow and Bertie Roddy who helped out with work around the flats.

Blocks and Shops
When the flats first opened in 1966 there were three blocks: the Rossville Street block, Joseph Street/Place block and the Fahan Street block. These contained around 157 apartments ranging from one bedroom to four bedrooms. There were three main walkways or floors used to access the flats across all the blocks and each of these floors had a name: the second floor was Garvan Place, the fifth floor Mura Place, and the eighth floor was Donagh Place. I always referred to them as the Rossville apartments although some people may not like that term being used.

There were two lifts (which were constantly broken) at the Rossville Street entrance to service the three balcony walkways. They were the only lifts you had for the three blocks. There were stairs at the side of those lifts and stairs at the very end of the Rossville Street block. The next set of stairs was at the Joseph Street side and another set at the top of Fahan Street. Because the flats were so high (approximately 120 feet) lightning conductors had to be installed even though at their highest point they were lower than nearby Butcher Gate on the Walls. There were only nine garages on the ground floor and 30 parking spaces to facilitate all the tenants.

There were several shops along the front of block two: McIntyre's butcher shop, Molly Barr's sweet and newspaper shop, Quinn's chemist, a playschool, and Hugh Quigley had a confectionery and greengrocer shop. There was also a Chinese restaurant/takeaway, which was very popular at the time. It was called The Sunflower and the proprietor was Tommy Ho from China. Next door to this was a supermarket and Doherty's bakery.

Troubled Times

The flats are famous for a lot of iconic things: the Battle of the Bogside, Bloody Sunday, and the hunger strike period. I was there during the hunger strikes when hijackings, bombings and shootings were common. A lot of rioting went on in and around the flats and it was common for people to throw stuff out the windows at the police or army. Some even claimed they saw a police Land Rover on Rossville Street with a cooker on top of it that was thrown from one of the flats. But this is probably just a good story.

Flight of the Cooker by Derry artist Locky Morris, 1987.

The British Army had a post and a helicopter landing point on the top of the flats and they carried out constant raids. We also had a few explosions in and around the flats and the army were attacked constantly. There were two soldiers killed in 1973 at the top floor so the army closed off the access point on the fifth floor. It was only accessible by them and us, the caretakers.

The lift room was up beside the army building. If someone got stuck in the lift we had to go up and manually move it to the next floor. We had to get access through the army and sometimes it was quite difficult as they were very reluctant to come down in case they were attacked. So it could take hours to get people out of the lifts; we often received verbal abuse when we eventually got them out! I had been up in the army living quarters as part of that role and they were in quite cramped conditions. They were living in a really enclosed area.

Community Spirit

It was trying times, but there were a lot of good families who lived there, a lot of camaraderie. It was a tragedy they had to knock the flats down. I think what happened was the majority of the flats were vacated due to damp conditions so they had to go.

We had some famous characters in the flats. There was Dickie Valley who had a big Alsatian called King, it was like a lion. Any time he mentioned Paisley it would go mental. Dickie claimed it was an ex-Securicor guard dog and was very ferocious. Then one day a small terrier dog came around the corner, King took one look at it and just turned and ran!

There was also Dickie McCarron whose house was very popular most nights for card schools for the local men. We had a former mayor of Derry, John Tierney, and Eurovision Song Contest winner Dana. Her father, Robert Brown, owned the barber shop at the front. We had a lot of famous people coming out of the flats.

I have very happy memories and, apart from the occasional bad times, there was great community spirit. We had a great family atmosphere in the flats and everybody got on really well. One of the great lines I always remember was, due to the rioting, that if there was nothing on the TV you could always just look out the window.

When they were knocked down the vast majority of residents moved into new properties in William Street, Brewster's Close, Lower Road and the Little Diamond area.

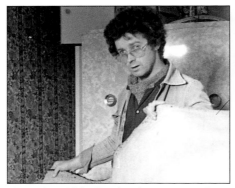

Caretaker Eddie Breslin demonstrates how bad the dampness was in some flats.

Philly Wilson goes waltzing with John Tierney.

Dickie Valley.

Moving In and First Impressions

The initial impressions of most of the families for their new housing in the Rossville Flats were positive, usually because they were moving from deteriorating terraced housing in the old Bogside with limited internal space, minimal washing facilities and basic outside toilets.

Eileen Collins
Given the standard of living that we were used to at the time, most people were happy with the flats. I lived in 20 Garvan Place, the very first unit above the shops on Joseph Place; it had two bedrooms, a living room, a kitchen and a small bathroom. There were also three- and four-bedroom flats and bedsits for the elderly and single people.

When I first moved in we were all new-fangled. Previous to that we didn't have an inside bathroom, we only had a toilet in the back yard. In my flat I walked in from the balcony and down a flight of stairs so although my front door was on the second floor I was actually on the first floor. The larger flats had two bedrooms downstairs and a toilet. Then they went up the stairs into the living area and another two bedrooms.

This was the first time that flats like these were built in Derry. Before this, people were used to houses. The flats were beautiful until the summer, then you were always sweating. They had very big windows so it was like a hot house in the summer and a fridge in the winter.

The row of shops which stood under block two on Joseph Place. At various times it housed: McIntyre's butcher shop, Molly Barr's sweet and newspaper shop, Quinn's chemist, a playschool, Brown's hair salon, Harley's chip shop, Sheerin's grocery, Hugh Quigley's confectionery and greengrocer shop, The Sunflower Chinese restaurant/take-away, a supermarket and Doherty's bakery among others.

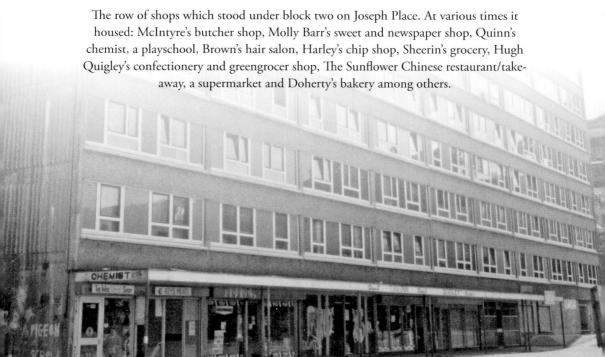

There was a bakery at the start and down from that was Joe Harley's chip shop where the Chinese takeaway moved into years later. There was Hugh Quigley's grocery shop (often called Danny's), Doherty's bakery and Molly Barr's newsagents for confectionery. Next door to Quigley's was Brown's hairdressers.

The Housing Trust had offices beside the shops, I remember paying my rent there. We had a few protests there, too, later on about the lack of facilities in the flats, the terrible conditions and how damp they were. Then the Housing Trust moved out and the community took over the space for youngsters to play table tennis. It was very small, not enough to facilitate the numbers of people who lived in the flats. That was in the early 1970s, just after the civil rights campaign started.

Above left: Hugh Quigley checks the till in his shop and
(above right) with a young customer.

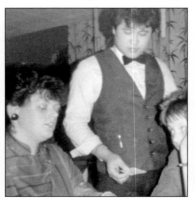

Above left: Sheila (Susan) Brown, Dana's mother, outside the family hairdressers. Above centre: Paul Ho serves Martha Doherty (née Long) and Catherine Long in his Sunflower Restaurant. Above right: Molly Barr with great-nephews and nieces Sean, Eileen, Seamus and Bernadette Barr.

Don Carlin

I loved it. It was a great start for Celine and me. We moved into the Joseph Street block which was for people who had no families. It was a one-bedroom up on the eighth floor with a kitchen, sitting room, bathroom and a toilet. Celine's parents and family were down on the second floor. That start we got in the flats was the best thing that ever happened to us. Luxury wasn't the word for it. It was as simple as that as far as I was concerned. It was what the people of the area needed.

Celine Carlin

I thought the flats were brilliant. If they were there today I'd still be there, providing it was my old neighbours that I went in with originally. The flats were just like one big happy family. The people used to go out and sit on the landings at night. You had your wains and as they were growing up you only had one door to worry about, put them to bed at night and there was no other way out, only the front door.

Sheila Brown

At first people were broken-hearted at having to move. But eventually they realised that the flats were comfortable and that there was good heating and there were good-sized bedrooms. They were so cheap to run as well. We were on the Joseph Street block and my mother was on the Rossville Street side. We realised we were living with old neighbours that we knew from the Bogside, people that we had been born and brought up with all our lives so we loved it.

To me it was like coming back to where I was brought up, where I was reared in 22 Union Street, off Rossville Street. When I was young, we had to go out to the toilet in the yard with a barrel and an outside tap. Many a night I was put out to wash my feet under the cold water tap. And then you had the tin enamel basins which you had to fill and bring in to wash the dishes. So when we moved to the

flats it was for the good although we didn't want to at first. My father cried his eyes out whenever they were forced to move, but there was nothing he could do about it. But most people really liked it once they got in.

It didn't worry me moving from a house to a high-rise flat because we were on the top floors which meant we only had to go around onto Fahan Street and we were on Butcher Street so it was very handy for us. I didn't have any real problems with it. Some of the others did not really like the height and would be always holding on as they went along the walkways.

At that particular time, people did not have very much choice in things, you just took what they gave you and accepted it and were glad to get it. Most people were very happy with their lot. Mrs McDermott from the Bogside was in a one-bedroom and she couldn't walk. There could have been a lot of things better for older people like her.

My daughter Eileen had just finished hairdressing training in Birmingham and I told her that they were going to build a row of shops underneath the flats so I suggested she rent one and she did. It was so big that her father did the gents at the front and she did the ladies at the back. That was on the Joseph Street side. Molly Barr was the first shop, then there was a chemist, next to that was Quigley's, the Wells had a grocer shop, and I think we were next to that.

Molly Barr's was the shop that everybody gathered in. We really loved Molly. We used to get everything there, she was full of craic and full of sport. There wasn't a lot else there I suppose and you just made do. Things were good at the start when we lived there but I don't know how the people managed when we left in 1971, it must have been hard going after that.

Philomena Wilson
Me and my husband and four children had a two-bedroom flat on Donagh Place on the eighth floor of the first Rossville Street block. Raymond was about eight, Sharon was seven, Catherine was six and Thomas was a baby. It was hard when the

Michael O'Neill poses on the bike as Elaine Ryan marches past.

lifts were off and there were more times they were broken than not. We lived there for three years until I got pregnant again when we moved to the second floor, a four-bedroom flat at 16 Garvan Place.

Some people who came from houses in the Bog with small rooms and outside toilets found it new-fangled to begin with, but they felt the flats were great. I thought it was absolutely marvellous because I had big bedrooms up the stairs and down and I had a bathroom and toilet, the sitting room was a good size, but the kitchen was small.

I loved the high flats. They were a new housing scheme and a lot of people were glad of them. If anybody asked at the time where I lived I would have said I'm from the multi-storey flats in the Bog. Some would be negative about them. But I would say they are the best place you could ever live in.

Martin Dunleavy
The flats were great, I had a good upbringing there. I always loved the flats until I started working on them. The first balcony we lived on was Garvan Place facing onto Rossville Street. We had great neighbours: the Currans, the Caseys, a whole team of them, McLaughlins, all good people. That was basically the early memories. We used to play football on the balconies and broke plenty of windows.

There were just two swings in the car park area for the children to play on. Later they opened up one of the disused shops for a children's playgroup. Other than that, there was nothing for the young kids.

Billy Carlin

We were in 8 Donagh Place on the top floor of the Rossville Street block. You went in the front door, onto the stairwell and then downstairs. Me and my brother Kevin shared the first bedroom until he left to join the Irish Army shortly after we moved in. My parents' room was next door and you had a toilet, a small bathroom, living room and a kitchen.

I was petrified at the start from just the pure height of the thing. I was never great with heights and am still not. I used to come across the balcony holding onto doors. I did that for quite a while before I got used to it. It would have been the first in terms of tower blocks for Derry and they came from all around to play in the flats, to the detriment of the older people I suppose.

Charlie McMenamin

I remember the day my grandparents, Charles and Kathleen Casey, moved from a terraced house in Nelson Street to 67 Mura Place in the Rossville Flats. This was the first flat as you came in from Waterloo Street/Fahan Street, just beside the Rocking Chair bar and directly opposite Butcher Gate.

Their home in Nelson Street had only four rooms, two up and two down, and an outside toilet. Washing, cleaning, bathing and cooking were all done in the backroom downstairs. Privacy was hard to get in those days. Myself and my uncle Terry carried bags of clothes and other bits and pieces over to the new flat from Nelson Street.

We were all new-fangled with the lift which would take us up to the fifth floor. The flat had two floors – upstairs there were four bedrooms, a walk-in cupboard and an airing cupboard. Downstairs had a bathroom, kitchen, sitting room, living room and another airing cupboard. It had a toilet upstairs and a toilet downstairs that you could flush, and a bath and hot water on tap all the time. All the rooms were very spacious and nowhere near as cramped as their house in Nelson Street. It was like moving to the lap of luxury.

Everyone moving into the flats seemed very happy. There was an air of contentment about them, with plenty of space for children to play and gas-fired central heating. It afforded the new residents a better standard of living compared to their previous dwellings. Coming from Howard Street myself, we lived in very cramped conditions and I decided from that day onwards that the flats were my new home – my grandparents (or Ma and Da as we called them) had no say in the matter. The flats were just like a big playground to me!

Martha McClelland
The flats weren't anything to look at when I first moved in. The flat I had was broken into and the door was hanging off. It was vandalised but not too badly. I was at number 25 Garvan Place, just over the wee shop. The bakery was at one end and the general shop was just below me.

There were funny things, too. There was a Chinese restaurant right next door to the shop. Sometimes, because I was on the first floor, people would get up on the roof of the Chinese and wander over to my window at two or three in the morning. There was always quite a lot of noise and disturbance there at night, but basically it was a great place to live.

Maureen Morrison

When the flats were being built we fought hard to get a move and were eventually offered accommodation at 38 Mura Place. It felt like a palace compared to what we were used to – we even had hot water and a bath! When we lived in Abbey Street we had to use the City Swimming Baths in William Street to get a bath which was better than the alternative; using a tin tub in the kitchen! It was also great to have proper heating – that was a real luxury.

Deirdre Conaghan

I moved into 22 Garvan Place in 1981 when I was 17. My twin brothers were born there, too. I raised my two boys there when I moved to 33 Garvan Place. When we lived there the flats were great craic, there was always something happening. We were just around the corner from the Rocking Chair bar which would have been my local then. It wasn't great for kids because of the riots and the balconies, but it was safe enough. My eldest boy Gavin had a go-kart toy and with his brother, Gareth, they used to fly around the balconies on it. It was the best thing I ever bought them. They had a ball.

Annette Harkin

I grew up in the flats. I always remember everybody's door being open. We lived on the eighth floor in 48 Donagh Place and there were nine of us in a two-bedroom flat. Everybody was like an aunt and uncle and you would have been in and out of everybody's flat.

Elaine and Annette Ryan.

Denise, Martina and Deborah O'Kane.

Sandra and Jacqueline Doherty
with Saoirse Ó Comáin.

Katrina McLoone and Caroline Doran.

Estate	Rossville Estate		Rent	from	Rent	from	Rent	from
Address	6, Donagh Place (9th floor)		28/-	9/5/66.				
Ref. No.	Type	P.L.V.						
	C a bd 1/4/67	£20 £18						

NAME OF TENANT (Surname)	(Christian Name)	Date of commencement of tenancy	Date of termination of tenancy	Past Tenant's Address
McFadden	Alexander	9/5/66.		

Alexander McFadden was one of the first residents to move into the flats in May 1966.

Estate	Rossville		Rent	from	Rent	from	Rent	from
Address	47, Donagh Place		28/-	30/10/67				
Ref. No.	Type 9th fl	P.L.V.	£ 18					
	C2Bd Block 2							

NAME OF TENANT (Surname)	(Christian Name)	Date of commencement of tenancy	Date of termination of tenancy	Past Tenant's Address
Lamberton	John	30/10/67		

John Lamberton moved into 47 Donagh Place in October 1967.

Estate	Rossville Estate, Londonderry		Rent	from	Rent	from	Rent	from
Address	18, Garvan Place		28/-	2/5/66.				
Ref. No.	Type 1/4/67	P.L.V. £18 £20						
	C1 2bd Bela- access gallery							

NAME OF TENANT (Surname)	(Christian Name)	Date of commencement of tenancy	Date of termination of tenancy	Past Tenant's Address
Patterson	David.	2/5/66		

David Patterson became a resident and the first caretaker in the flats in May 1966.

Estate	Rossville, Londonderry		Rent	from	Rent	from	Rent	from
Address	67, Mura Place		37/6	8/5/67				
Ref. No.	Type	P.L.V. £26						
	D2 N A1 S 2nd & 3rd floor							

NAME OF TENANT (Surname)	(Christian Name)	Date of commencement of tenancy	Date of termination of tenancy	Past Tenant's Address
CASEY,	CHARLES	8/5/67		

Charles Casey moved into 67 Mura Place in May 1967.

Gaslight Company payment records from 1970.

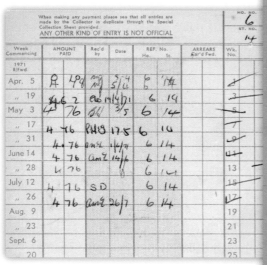

THE LONDONDERRY GASLIGHT COMPANY

METER CARD

Ref. No.

Please keep this Card clean and close to the Meter

THIS CARD MUST BE PRODUCED WHEN A COLLECTION IS MADE

Consumers are requested to see that each entry made is correct

The only official entry is that made by the Collector in duplicate through the Special Collection Sheet provided

This Payment Card is the property of the Company. If lost or mislaid, a charge of ONE SHILLING will be made to the Consumer

Housing Trust Rent Card of Alexander McFadden from 1972.

35

Good Neighbours and Community Spirit

Despite the basic amenities, lack of facilities and increasingly poor housing conditions, the tenants always remarked on how much they enjoyed living and socialising with good neighbours, many of whom came from the same old streets in the Bogside they had previously shared. The strong community spirit that emerged and grew in the flats is testament to the depth of character and positive outlook of people who had endured ongoing deprivation, discrimination and inequality over many decades in the city.

Philomena Wilson
I felt it was a family all together. If you needed a neighbour you hadn't a problem. I could have walked around at any time of night, no matter what was going on or what was happening, and I felt very secure in the high flats.

My neighbours used to come and go. John Dunleavy was the caretaker, Marie Meenan and Sadie Redden lived beside me. Eileen McCrudden would have been very extravagant because she had a cat called Tiddles or something. I would have spent a lot of time with Mary Lamberton and Anne Tierney. I would have went up to their place and just sat

Davy Patterson, the first caretaker of the Rossville Flats.

outside on the balcony to three or four in the morning. At that time we wouldn't have taken a drink, but the craic would have been 90. There were others I got to know such as Eileen Collins and Kathleen Wallace, Marie Johnson, Celine Carlin, the Ryans and John Tierney.

Martha McClelland
It was great living in the flats. The people were great, I have a lot of nice memories of the people; the camaraderie, the people going up and down the stairs. All your friends were very close by and that was a source of a lot of good memories. People were very tolerant.

I can think of one negative thing about my neighbours, though. Somebody above me used to throw down bags of rubbish and they would land on the roof of the shop just outside my window. I always used to get these marrowfat peas. If I could find those people I would hang them or throttle them to death.

Don Carlin

It was great that everybody mucked in with one another. If anything was wrong the usual people helped out. I remember us on the second-floor walkway with maybe 20 or 30 neighbours all sitting with chairs and sofas. You name it, it was brought out and everybody was sitting back and smoking and one thing and another. A few of the women would have gone in and made tea, brought it out maybe with buns and biscuits. We would be there to two or three in the morning, sitting back and having a bit of craic. That was the beauty of the flats. You would have got the odd one that complained, there's always somebody who gets annoyed.

When we first moved in, Davy Patterson was the caretaker and he was great at his job. If you didn't live in the flats you didn't get into that lift. He'd ask, 'Do you live in the flats? No? Well out you go!' They would have had to walk round past Molly Barr's shop and go up the steps to take you into Fahan Street between the flats and Joseph's Place. Davy used to say, 'That's how you do it, you're not coming in here to use the lifts.'

Celine Carlin

At that time, if one woman was pregnant nearly the whole flats were pregnant. We used to blame Billy Doherty's buns for it. One particular year, among the wains born were Roy Wilson, Donna Tierney, Aisling Ferguson and Martin Johnson.

Kathleen Casey with grandson Frankie McMenamin and his cousin Lisa, 1976.

Paddy O'Hagan with his son Kevin, 1981.

John Lamberton, John Tierney, Brian Tierney, Mary Lamberton (née Tierney), Ann Ryan (née Tierney), Martina Gillan (née Coyle) with Julie Dunlop (née Lamberton) on her first communion.

Billy, Jean and John Friel.

Colum McConomy.

Marriage of Paddy O'Hagan and Teresa McMenamin in 1980. The reception was held in Kathleen Casey's Mura Place flat.

Includes Nicky Carter, Tibs Murphy, Gareth Bradley, Eamon Carlin, Gary O'Neill, Trevor Lamberton, Gareth Hamilton and Colum Bradley.

Robert Strain and friend.

Charles, Mary and Terry Lamberton.

Jim (Doc) Doherty, Cathy Doherty (née Kerrigan) and Gael Doherty.

Bernie and Donna Tierney with Aisling and Sean Ferguson and friends.

You also had Owen McGarrigle and one of the Kinetons (my ma and my da stood for him). Trevor Lamberton was born that year, too, and one of Ann Ryan's. I was the last of the bunch and I had Eileen.

On our landing we had Patsy Fox, Tommy McGavigan, Patsy Irvine, Mrs Boyle, Lily McConomy, Kitty Fox, Colm O'Kane, and Billy Harley. You had 'Red Boots' Hasty as we called him, and May McFadden, originally from Nelson Street, Minnie Pickett, Mary Lamberton and Ann Ryan.

Sheila Brown

I really loved living in the flats. But I know there were other people who felt different. You remember all the bad days and all the good days as well. Whatever was happening with everybody we could go out and laugh with our neighbours. I used to love the wee knock at the door and there they were coming in for a visit or cup of tea. Even if you were sitting by yourself, you weren't really on your own.

Charlie McMenamin

It was a great community, the people were really friendly and helpful to each other, and they all came from the surrounding streets. You could say the flats became a focal point, a microcosm of the Troubles. If anything happened in the flats, everybody was out because everybody was in the middle of it.

Back: Harry Jones, Edmund Houston, Patsy McCauley and Hugh McCauley. Front: James McConnell, Hugh McConnell, John Harkin, Michael McConnell and Tracy McCauley.

The sense of community we had in the high flats, I would love to have it back again. You make a lot of mistakes in life, but you don't learn unless you make mistakes, and that's where I made most of my mistakes, in the high flats.

Billy Carlin

On the right-hand side of us were the Friels – John, Joan, Bap, Mary, Bernie, Sheila and Leo, there were quite a few Friels. Joan Doherty had wee Tojo and a daughter. John Tierney, the former mayor, lived a couple of doors up and he had a host of wains. And around the other side, the Ryans and the Meenans, they were all very young families. You weren't talking two or three to a family, you're talking big families.

The first band I ever played with rehearsed in a wee 'club' on the fifth floor. James Downey from Abbey Park on guitar, Annette Divin from Lisfannon Park on guitar, a fella from Creggan called Alex Long on the drums and me doing the singing. We rehearsed a lot, but nothing ever came of it.

Some great musicians came out of the flats, like the McCauley brothers and Don Carlin who drummed with some of the best bands around in his day. The McConnell brothers, Jackie and Seamus, played with some of the biggest showbands at that time, the Plattermen and bands like that. Johnny McCauley, probably one of the best guitarists to come out of the town, was sought after by all the showbands as well.

The Friel family, circa 1982: Tony, Amanda, Leo, Bernadette, Billy, Jean and Mary.

Bridie, Sean and Aisling Ferguson with the 'Hulk', Billy Carlin.

Emmett and Donna Tierney with Raymond, Melissa, Brian and Elaine Ryan.

Left: The McGinley family: Michael, Sean, Raymond, Sarah, John, Irene, Ann and Siobhan.

Young members of the Goode family and friends.

Includes Pat Ramsey, John Tierney, Mickey Deery, Damien Doherty, Katrina McLoone (née Rouse), Nana McGilloway (née Lamberton), Tommy Warren, Mary Lamberton (née Tierney), May Carlin, Raymond Ryan, Willie Rouse, Chris Ramsey (née Harkin), Ann Ryan (née Tierney), Nancy Meenan (née White) and Philly Wilson (née McMenamin).

Hugh O'Neill and Gerald Coyle.

Patsy Irwin with son Roland alongside Philomena Irwin (née Murphy) with sons Bryan and Trevor.

I remember summer nights up in the eighth floor, pulling out the guitar and the next thing you would have 30 or 40 people around you having a sing-song. And then somebody would land with a carry-out and you would have partied on all night. Wee things like that happened every now and again, the craic was good.

Everybody was there for one another. No matter what happened there was always somebody there to comfort you or get some help if needed from elsewhere, maybe just offer a loaf of bread or a bag of sugar. Or if a family was really hard up, the neighbours would have organised a collection and got some groceries in for them. Nobody really felt their pride was hurt by accepting help, people just got on with things, the community spirit was definitely there.

People kept their wee flats like palaces, everybody left their door on the latch. You could just walk in and out of people's homes and people felt grand about it. I never heard of any of the flats being broken into or anybody getting stuff stolen from them because everybody seemed to be in each other's pocket anyway. I think you knew not to do anything because people would have just turned on you, especially if you lived there. If an outsider had tried anything dodgy I dread to think what would have happened.

Annette Harkin
The flats were like our own town. There was much more positive than there was negative, there was great community spirit. On a Saturday night everybody would sit out on the balcony and people would sing; my mother was a great singer. It was just like a big sing-song.

Deirdre Conaghan
There was a great sense of community and everybody was there for each other. If something was going on you could always depend on your neighbours.

Notable Events and Memorable People

Like any community, the Rossville Flats had numerous generous or kind-hearted residents who were acknowledged and respected for their contribution to, and selfless support of, others. It also had its share of talented or 'interesting' people who will always be remembered for providing colour, entertainment and much-needed levity at times.

Sheila Brown

I was over in Amsterdam with my mother and Rosemary [Dana] when she won the Eurovision Song Contest in 1970. Robert did not go over. I remember Mary Hopkins was on before her and she was excellent and I said to my mother, it's either Rosemary or Mary Hopkins. Rosemary was lucky enough. Me and my mother sat down at the back and never went up near it when she won. Everybody was rushing mad up to the stage but we just sat there and never bothered.

I wondered would they know back in Derry and if anybody would be there to meet us when we got home. But when we got the length of Dublin there were thousands there to see her. They put a special plane on for us to Dublin and then to Ballykelly, and when we landed we saw all the people and the cars, it was unbelievable. We had a reception at the Guildhall and then we went back to the flats. There were crowds everywhere, but we got Rosemary in and up the back stairs. They called for Rosemary to sing *All Kinds Of Everything* and she sung it from the balcony.

Rosemary Brown (Dana) and Father Carlin.

Father Edward Daly joins the celebrations for Dana's Eurovision success.

They came from all parts of the world to our flat to do interviews. Everybody was out, it was definitely a big event, not only for people who lived in the flats but people who came from Derry and Ireland. It's like a dream to us now that it happened, but the people were marvellous, the people were great, I could not believe it that they were there in such big numbers.

Don Carlin

I remember Bernard O'Neill, God rest him. Bernard, maybe on a Friday or Saturday night, would go to the pub and have a few jars and he would stand out on the balcony and let rip with a few songs. I thought it was brilliant. Everybody would have joined him. I would have said, 'Come on, Bernard, give us another one.' He would have been singing away. It was absolutely brilliant.

Eileen Collins

Dickie Valley was an inoffensive being. I remember once after the rioting, it was really bad, they were down looting in Sackville Street. Dickie come up to my mother's and said, 'Mrs Shiels, do you want a kettle, iron, toaster or washing machine? What do you want? I'll get it for you now when the chance is good.'

There was a story went out about him that one time he went up to Scott's jewellery shop in the Diamond when it was on fire. After the firemen put it out, the ladders were still up against the building and Dickie was caught inside filling his pockets with jewellery. The Brit said, 'What are you doing here? Who are you?' Dickie said, 'I'm an insurance assessor.'

Then you had Johnny Pine, he was another character. He would have been a friend of Dickie's. He was a very smart man. He used to write letters into the *Journal* long before the civil rights movement came into being in Derry. He wrote about the conditions in Derry, about the bad situation in the city. Ordinary people never took the letters on, but he saw things happening that nobody saw.

Billy Carlin

Dickie Valley who lived with Evelyn was legendary in the town. He was always winding everybody up with his yarns and things he got up to. Dickie would have told you stories like the time he claimed he swam from near the Star factory on Foyle Road towards the Boat House in Prehen with a gas cooker on his back! He would tell you he was about 15 yards from the far side, but he couldn't make it all the way so had to turn back. You would have been standing with your mouth open in disbelief saying: 'For God's sake, you went 500 yards just to turn back, sure you could have made the 15 yards.' Then the penny would drop and you knew you were caught.

I remember one time he came to our flat and complained to my mother about us all playing knick-knock on the doors. He said, 'I'll put the knick-knocking out of them!' So he went and wired up the light socket next to his door to his letterbox and threw a bucket of water on the ground outside the door. Tony Strain went up and grabbed the letterbox to knock and he was stuck to it for about three minutes with the shock. Dickie came out then and hit him a quare clash as well. You would never forget things like that. There was some craic went on in the flats.

Philomena Wilson

Don Carlin would have been a character in the flats. Mr Ryan, too. No matter what child went to the door, they knew they would get a biscuit or something and he would have fed quite a few children. May Carlin would have been a character. If anybody important was coming to visit May was out scrubbing the balconies so we all had to start scrubbing and making a ring around our front door, which I would have been well used to out in St Columb's Wells. Another character would have been Joan Doherty. She was from Liverpool and as soon as Joan saw the police or army she would have been out barging.

Dickie Valley was a wile man. He would have done anything for you, no matter what you would have wanted, he definitely was a great character. I knew him from St Columb's Wells. Another character would have been Lily Frazier, an older woman who lived on the eighth floor. She used to come out at night singing steady and one of her favourites was *Sock It To Me, Baby*.

Even if people didn't have a lot, they all chipped in together. Annie O'Neill and them, she would have done a wile lot for children in the flats and she wasn't paid for it. She would take them on bus runs, have parties for them. She would have been a spokesperson at times for us if anything was going wrong in the flats. Good people.

Martha McClelland

The Bogside Republican Youth (BRY) were great I have to admit, although sometimes I'd like to wring their necks. When you find petrol bombs on the stairs, just left there, and youngsters playing with matches; things like that weren't very good, but most of the time the BRY were very courteous. Once, when my motorbike was parked up at the kerb near where they were planning an attack on the RUC or the army, I came back from working at the Sinn Féin centre to find they had moved it inside to the hallway, so they could throw the petrol bombs without damaging my motorbike. They didn't want to incorporate it into the war effort. I thought that was very considerate.

Terry Lamberton

When I was at primary school, everyone lived for the summer holidays, mainly because they seemed to last forever. The big event in many areas was the annual 15 August bonfire. After the middle of July the young people in the flats would start collecting wood and tyres for the fire. We had a big advantage as there were so many children living in the flats and with the Troubles a lot of the buildings in the William Street area were lying derelict. We were able to get a lot of old wooden beams from them for the fire.

When looking for tyres, we had to go down onto the quay. The first garage we came to is now a well-known restaurant, Quaywest. If we didn't get any tyres there, we went further down the quay to another garage with a scrapyard near it. There was a garage at the bottom of the Rock Road which was the best place for getting big lorry or tractor tyres. When we got any of these back to the flats, children would play with them by getting inside the tyre and being pushed around and around by their friends. Most of the tyres were kept in people's flats or stores until bonfire night so they wouldn't be stolen by boys from other streets. All the different areas would be trying to steal stuff for their own bonfire and we always had to fight off the nearest gang from Abbey Street. In the end, it became just entertainment for everyone rather than any serious rows.

On the big day, everything was brought to the middle of the car park to build the bonfire. When it was lit crowds would gather round and residents came out onto the balconies with chairs to sit and watch. People often said it was the biggest bonfire in the town. Wuzz Doherty said he could even see the flames over the top of the flats from Celtic Park!

Martha McClelland
addresses a gathering
in the Bogside.

Bogside Republican
Youth members at a
vehicle checkpoint
on Rossville Street.

Collecting for the bonfire at the back of the flats.

Sean Ryan, John Tierney and friends help out with the bonfire.

A mini-barricade of old tyres helps protect the bonfire in the middle of Rossville Street as local youths gather more material for the big night.

Stephen Ryan

One of the main things I remember about growing up in the Rossville Flats was when you finished school in the summer you collected for the bonfires. There was me and Eddie Meenan. I think Sean McCarthy was there although he didn't live in the flats. We were about nine at the time. Before Pilot's Row was built there was a waste ground there. Every day when you were collecting you got bits and pieces and made a wee tiny fire. This day we wanted to burn an armchair. Billy Canning was sitting on it and everybody tried to get him off it. We tried everything. There was a crowd of us and we tried to lift him off. All he did to keep us from burning the armchair was to just sit in it. We couldn't get burning that day. We ended up having to stone him, but we still didn't get burning it. That was the life. The only thing you did when you left school was collect for the bonfires.

Role of the Rossville Flats
in the Battle of the Bogside

During the Battle of the Bogside between 12–14 August 1969, dozens of people occupied the roof of the Rossville Flats and used it as a key vantage point from which to bombard the RUC with petrol bombs and missiles of all description in an effort to keep them from overwhelming the area. On the last day of the battle, as the RUC and B-Specials were gathering for another attack, British soldiers, who had just been sent to the North, made their way between the warring factions in the Bogside. The RUC and B-Specials withdrew and the historic battle came to an end.

Thomas McCourt

The flats weren't that important in the earlier stages of the street disturbances in Derry. But they really came to prominence in the Battle of the Bogside, that was really how it all started. We were involved in the Young Socialists at that time and we were trying to run various kinds of campaigns and demonstrations and one of the things that came up was running a radio station, which became Radio Free Derry. We sourced one in Belfast and I remember picking it up in a bar in Toomebridge. It was a wee small thing. I expected a big aerial but it was just a wee box so we had to figure out what we were going to do with it. Eventually, somebody gave us advice on the length of the aerial and how to work it so we managed to get it up and running.

We decided to try and set the radio up so that it was operating on the day of the annual Apprentice Boys celebration march so we put it in a flat which was overlooking Rossville Street. I couldn't tell you whose flat it was, but if you went up the front entry it would have been maybe three flats to the left down along Rossville Street, one of the top flats. We ran the aerial out the window and out onto the roof so when it broke I had to go up in through the lift shaft and onto the roof of the flats to fix it. At that time there was nobody on the roof of the flats as the rioting hadn't started. I could see the marchers on the city Walls. I remember hanging our aerial on the large TV aerial which was on the roof to service all the flats. We ran one length of the aerial from there up towards Joseph's Place and the other length down the roof along Rossville Street, at right angles to each other. The connector lead hung down the front of the flats from the top storey.

Radio Free Derry kept people informed, and entertained, during the Battle of the Bogside.

We were broadcasting when we heard a fella called Seth (who was a friend of Bernadette Devlin) who was on the roof with a walkie-talkie. There was another walkie-talkie in William Street. I had my head out the window and Seth was shouting: 'They're gathering down at the end of Rossville Street.' And the next thing he starts shouting: 'They're rioting, the cops are baton charging!' So in turn I was broadcasting on Radio Free Derry, shouting and trying to tell people what was going on. I remember looking down from the flats and seeing a group of people who I recognised as being in the Young Socialists and they were standing around a transistor radio. I was broadcasting: 'I am calling all the Young Socialists, build the barricades.' I could see them all looking around and I was shouting at them over the airwaves: 'Don't be looking around, build the barricades.' And they were stunned at the fact that their every move was being watched, but that was the kind of craic that happened.

When the cops made a baton charge up Rossville Street everybody assumed the worst was going to happen. People got frightened that if they came in and up the stairs everybody would have been trapped in the flats. Everyone panicked so I pulled the aerial out of the radio and in the window and then all I saw was a whole shower of delft, TVs, anything really that was portable, was landing on the heads of the police. I realised then we had panicked too soon, that the cops weren't going to make it into the flats, so we connected up the radio again. At that stage the radio

station became irrelevant, the rioting was the most important thing and everybody headed out to join in.

I couldn't actually tell you who were the first up on the roof to start using it as a good place to defend the area. I had been up there with the aerial and I remember going back up again and there was only a handful there. People were arguing about how to get up and some were even talking about going out the window. But I knew the lift shaft was a safer way so before long there were maybe a hundred people on the roof.

There was very little on the roof that you could throw, so bottles were getting passed up, petrol bombs, box loads of stones. Boys were landing up with these great ideas, rubber tubes trying to make catapults and all sorts. Everybody was over mainly at the far Rossville Street corner.

The RUC were firing CS gas up so there was a sort of transient population with people heading down and coming up again, it was all hectic. Every time a canister landed on the roof it was just pandemonium. I recall a younger boy, I am nearly sure it was Brian Deehan, who was temporarily blinded with the gas making a mad panicked run. He would have gone over the edge, but I managed to grab him and pull him down to the ground and him squealing because the gas was in his face.

Sean Sheils brought a tricolour and an American flag up onto the roof on the first day. We put up the tricolour and I remember shouting at somebody to get a Starry Plough flag. I remember arguing that the tricolour and the Starry Plough were okay but there was a big row about the American flag. Sean was arguing the propaganda value of the Brits being seen attacking the Stars and Stripes. Being one of the Young Socialists, I was arguing that we were not going to fight under the imperialist flag of a nation whose soldiers were killing people in Vietnam. So the American flag was discarded.

We stayed up there for the guts of the three days. Afterwards, we put the radio up on top of the lift shaft itself. It was there for maybe four or five weeks and I used

Community activists Bernadette Devlin and Nell McCafferty strongly supported the resistance on the streets as the RUC made repeated attempts to enter and subdue the area.

to go up and broadcast. I remember British journalists coming over and asking us about this radio – they thought it was like the French Resistance or something – and me taking them up the lift shaft and, foolishly I suppose, showing them where the radio was. They wanted to record somebody talking live so I used to go up and start into all these silly talks when the radio wasn't even switched on.

I would have been on the radio fairly regularly, but there were others who took a turn presenting such as Seamus O'Kane, 'Hookie' McDermott and Eamonn McCann who would have done an odd piece on it. Joe Quigley would have done

Members of the RUC made a stand at the corner of Rossville Street and William Street and some hurled missiles in retaliation.

a bit and the Young Socialists would have been working very closely with the Officials. People like Johnny White, Mickey Montgomery and Eamon Melaugh among others would have been on air occasionally.

Charlie McMenamin

The worst rioting was during the Battle of the Bogside in August 1969. People were running in and out of the flats with petrol bombs and stones and every time the B-Specials made a snatch to try to catch rioters my granny's hall filled up with people. As usual there was always more spectators than rioters.

As things worsened, my grandparents talked more and more about their fears for members of their family and their resolve to stay on and protect their home at any cost. My grandparents wouldn't send me home at this time because where we lived was under siege from Loyalists and members of the B-Specials. A barricade had been built outside our house in Howard Street to protect the area so I was no better off going home, not that I would have wanted to. I was enjoying all the excitement.

It all came to a head on the third night. We were all sitting in the dark watching the rioting between a crowd of youngsters on Fahan Street and the RUC and some marchers on the Walls. My granny decided it best to close her venetian blinds when the two sitting-room windows came in on top of us, showering the whole room with glass. Fortunately enough the curtains took most of the impact.

I was shifted out of the flats that night and ended up in a house in Foyle Road belonging to a family called Patterson. My mother had already been evacuated to Foyle Road also from Howard Street with the rest of the family.

Eileen Collins

I have very vivid memories of the Battle of the Bogside. In those days, milk and lemonade were sold in bottles which were all kept. People would fill the bottles with petrol from cars and take them up to the top of the flats in crates to throw at the RUC. All sorts and ages were on the roof over the three days. There were middle-aged men and women. And teenagers. Literally everybody there.

A blanket of CS gas just hung over everything at times. Anyone with chest problems at all, well, it would have killed them, I would say it's only coming out now how it was affecting people. I think there was some kind of survey that showed that more people died with cancer in the Derry area than any other part of the six counties as a result of that time.

We had to take the children into the bathroom or they would be very sick because there were no windows but the gas was coming in through a little vent. It got so bad we took the youngsters over the border. We were lucky my mother had a caravan in Donegal. A lot of people had nowhere to go, they had to go to army camps out of the town altogether.

Bloody Sunday Remembered

On 30 January 1972, a march to protest against internment changed everything – not just in Derry where it took place, but across the country and beyond. For everyone living in Derry at the time, Bloody Sunday will remain long in the memory as probably the most heartbreaking and significant event of the Troubles.

The 1st Battalion of the Parachute Regiment shot 26 people on that day, resulting in 14 deaths. This took place in the wider shadow of the Rossville Flats and one of the deceased, Hugh Gilmour, was a resident there. This terrible massacre of innocent civilians by the British Army – which many witnessed either on the streets outside or from their windows – greatly affected all those who lived in the flats.

Eileen Collins
Bloody Sunday was a very sad memory. It started out a beautiful day. I arranged with my nephew, Eamonn, to look after the wee ones for me. I warned him not to let them out of the flats because after every march there was always a mini riot. Me and a neighbour went up to Creggan where the march started. The march got as far as William Street when the first shot rang out. I saw a man being carried away and that was my cue to move. I went to my mother's house and helped to treat some injured people there for nearly an hour. But when I wanted to leave to go back to the youngsters I couldn't, the army was everywhere.

The British soldiers were cursing and roaring out of them. I saw a whole squad of people being arrested and marched down with their hands behind their heads, among them was Father Bradley. Eventually it got a wee bit quieter and I got out of my mother's and I ran down Columcille Court. I saw a fella being carried into the Carrs' house and I went in. There were two or three bodies there and I was really in nerves then about the youngsters. I went down through Kells Walk and a British soldier stopped me, he told me I wasn't allowed down. I said, 'I have to get down, my youngsters are in the flat on their own.' I ran on down and when I think of it now I could have been shot.

When I went into the flats it was desperate. Around the flats the wee fella Gilmour's blood was still running and Barney McGuigan was just being taken away in an ambulance. Hugh Gilmour was a nice wee fella, just your normal Derryman. He was never involved in anything.

I went up into my flat. We had a big press in the living room where the meter was and the youngsters were all in there. The two bigger boys were in convulsions and the two wee ones were not really aware of what was going on. Eamonn was in a wile state. I got them settled and we were watching out the window when somebody shouted up to stay well back because they were still shooting. All you could see were jeeps and 'pigs' and ambulances. Free Derry Corner was just facing me and I could see people coming out from hiding and you knew they were afraid. Everything went dead quiet. The rumours were coming in about how many had been shot dead. It wasn't until the 9 o'clock news that night that the full story came out. It was a very bad time.

Don Carlin

Bloody Sunday was a terrible experience. One of the worst things that ever happened in Derry. I was at the march with my brother-in-law, he got stuck between the barricade at the Rossville Street side and the entrance of the flats. There were a lot of bricks flying around. I crawled out on my belly and grabbed him by the scruff of the neck and I pulled him into the main entrance of the flats. I think I was the last person that Hugh Gilmour spoke to because I was standing at the flats when Hugh went around the corner and he said to me, 'I'm hit, Don, I'm hit.' I'll never forget that till the day I die. There was another young fella, Kevin McElhinney, lying on the first floor of the stairs. The poor fella was dead. It was crazy that day.

There was no atmosphere around the place in the days after, just a deathly silence all over the whole area. When you went out to see what was happening there were groups of mostly men standing about. Usually there's always a conversation, about football, dogs, horses or whatever. But there was nothing, not a thing.

British troops stormed the Bogside and detained dozens of bystanders, many of whom were trying to help the injured and dying.

Philomena Wilson

Things turned bad after Bloody Sunday. I was pregnant at the time and I was out on the march with Nancy Meenan and my sister-in-law. We just got to the high flats and the crowd was so big I just thought I'll go on in home now when they opened up. I mind running up to Nancy's flat and when I looked out the first person I saw dead was Paddy Doherty. I don't know whether it was nerves, but I ran out again and down the back stairs and over to him. I never saw so much blood and I went into Molly Barr's. Hugh Gilmour was killed as well and he lived in the flats. He was only 17. I knew him and his family well. After that happened it was very wet the whole night long. There was just that dreary feeling the whole way through. We expected the army to come back in to do a lot more damage, I was terrified.

Martin Dunleavy

I didn't experience Bloody Sunday myself, I was only five, but I remember being in Creggan and growing up with the atmosphere after Bloody Sunday. It was more frightening than anything because at that age, I was only six or seven, you saw gun battles every day basically. We used to be able to sit in the flats and watch boys and girls across the street in Kells Walk and Glenfada Park. There were gun battles steady between Rossville Street and the roof of the Embassy.

I think everybody wised up to that after Bloody Sunday. Everybody knew the danger then. Bloody Sunday changed everything.

My mother worked in a shirt factory until she had to retire through ill health. Bloody Sunday stuck in her mind. She didn't go on the march. She had her coat on and off three times to go to the meeting at Free Derry Corner but decided not to. The shooting started and she decided to go up and see if she could see my brother who was on the march. She said that she had just stepped out and saw Jackie Duddy running through the courtyard of the flats. She saw Father Daly running in front of him. Just the minute she stepped out onto the balcony, Jackie Duddy swung round. He was shot in the back and the soldier that shot him swung the rifle up and pointed it at my mother standing at her front door. She stepped back into the flat. That was the only thing my mother ever really talked about in the Rossville Flats.

There would be something seriously wrong if these things didn't have an effect on you. There are things you never forget, no matter what age you are. It lives with you till the day you die.

Frankie McMenamin

I walked along Rossville Street on Monday morning, the day after Bloody Sunday, with my mother, brothers and sisters towards the Rossville Flats where my granny

Casey lived. I was only eight years old. As we approached the flats I could see blood stains and shoes scattered across the streets. I could see people standing all around and children kneeling down praying beside the blood stains. Many people were standing around crying amidst what seemed like an eerie silence. I did not understand what was going on, after all, I was only an eight-year-old. I did not know what had happened on the day before; the day that became known as Bloody Sunday.

I asked my mother what was going on. She told me that 'bad men' had killed some people the day before. Trying to make sense of it, I kept looking at the blood and the shoes on the streets as she took us towards the flats. The only death I had experienced was on the television. I asked her where the dead people had gone. My mother told me that God and the angels had come down and lifted the people to heaven from the place where their bodies lay. I wondered why people did not get into heaven with their shoes on.

I do not remember much afterwards about Bloody Sunday although my mother and father took us to the funerals. I remember trying to understand what was in the wooden boxes if the people had already gone to heaven. All I do know about that day is that something died in our community. Things never seemed the same again.

The impact of Bloody Sunday can be felt to this day. The sad but understandable thing is that you can still see the pain that the families still live with; that of losing a family member – a father, a brother, a son, an uncle or close friend. The people killed that day were just ordinary people who took to the streets for their civil rights and better living conditions that had been denied to the people for many, many years.

People sought shelter from the gunfire while others treated the wounded
in and around the Rossville Flats.

Rossville Flats' resident Hugh Gilmour (above, third from left)
who was shot and killed on Bloody Sunday.

Several bullet holes are visible in the window of a second-floor flat from shots fired by
members of the British Army on Bloody Sunday.

Coping in Troubled Times

The British Army first appeared on the streets of Derry on 14 August 1969 to end the Battle of the Bogside between the RUC and local residents. They were initially welcomed by a majority of the weary but triumphant inhabitants who had been resisting the RUC for three days. But not everyone was happy to see them. Before long, the reception turned sour, perceptions changed and a more vicious phase of the conflict emerged with rioting and gun battles erupting on a regular basis.

The residents of the flats were greatly impacted when the army occupied the roof after Operation Motorman in July 1972 and commandeered some storage space on the adjoining storey for their living quarters. They maintained a presence there into the early 1980s. The substantial damage they did to the roof led to increased dampness in the flats and the security measures they imposed for their

safety caused constant disruption, worry and stress for the residents. The army and RUC also mounted regular raids on the flats, often resulting in widespread damage to people's property and possessions which only added to the tension for the residents who had no option but to cope with it all as best they could.

Deirdre Conaghan
Our flat was raided at one point when I was there with three young children, my brothers and my son. The army came in and the wains had to be lifted out of the cot. There was a whole big thing around it afterwards and it was featured in the local newspapers.

When I lived in Garvan Place there was rioting one night and the bullets were bouncing off the walls around our windows. I had to sit on the staircase with my son, I was terrified. That was the scary side being so close to the riots which were raging at the time.

Opposite top: A British Army helicopter lands on the roof of the flats to resupply the soldiers in the observation post.

Opposite and below: Operation Motorman gets underway in July 1972.

Above and below: The 1970s and '80s witnessed ongoing street disturbances on the streets of Derry and the high flats were a central feature in the turmoil of the times.

Troops secure the area to allow the safe evacuation of one of their men after he and a fellow soldier were caught in a bomb blast on the eighth floor in November 1984.

Martin Dunleavy

A woman on the top floor on Fahan Street was shot one night during a gun battle. I remember her being taken out of the flat into the ambulance and the apron she was wearing actually ended up in our flat for some reason. It was soaked in blood. She had been shot in the arm or in the top part of the body.

My sister was caught up in a gun battle once in the flats. They were shooting from the eighth floor and she was coming up the stairs with one of our cousins. They must have been trapped for about half an hour with the bullets bouncing all around them.

A lot of dodgy stuff went down the chute if the army or police came in. The RUC actually caught on to what was happening so they would go straight for the chutes when they came in to search. One time in the late 1970s there was a bomb being made in the flats. The army came in raiding the place so the people making it dumped it down the chute.

A couple of times my da was seriously caught up in bombings. One was underneath the stairs at the lifts at Rossville Street. The army were raiding that day, police and army were all over the place. My da was standing in the middle of them because he always wanted to watch that they weren't wrecking lifts or whatever. They were standing watching him and the bomb went off. It scared the shit out of the whole lot of them. My da was that close that day, too. Some of the soldiers pulled their pistols out and started pointing them at my da. They thought he had triggered it when he was standing in the middle of them.

After a bomb attack around the ground-floor lifts, the army seal off the area to enable their follow-up investigation.

There were many sad times. Like the hunger strikes and the day in 1982 when wee Stephen McConomy was killed with a plastic bullet in Fahan Street. Bloody Sunday obviously, too. Many people got killed or badly injured in or around the flats.

In 1984 there was a bomb in a flat and two soldiers were seriously injured. Some reckon they died. The army always had a policy of not admitting to all their casualties. My da actually managed to get up to the eighth floor in the lift that day. He saw the two soldiers lying outside the flat. One of them was still alive, but he had a leg blown off. He didn't know about the other one. I remember them bringing the two soldiers down. That night there was a lot of commotion.

Shortly after the bomb attack, the army came in for a full-blown raid. It went on for four or five days continuously. They made some excuse that they had found an IRA house or flat and they arrested somebody for it as well. They just went through the whole place. They didn't give a monkey's. They just carved through.

My da was involved in a lot of hairy stuff.

Annette Harkin

The army played a big part in life at the flats. They had observation posts on the roof. At the start, we used to go down to the shop for the soldiers and get them the paper, chocolate and fruit etc. But when the Troubles started we were told we weren't allowed to do it anymore and then they started deliberately sticking the lift on us.

There was us (the Ryans), the Lambertons, the O'Neills, the Meenans, and we all used to go and do drama at Pilot's Row. On our way home once the army stuck the lift on us and we were all trapped inside for three hours. The fire brigade had to come and get it open.

I remember the police coming into our flat and raiding it. I remember a lot of fellas up on the roof throwing washing machines and whatever else they could get off the building and down onto the police and army. I can remember rioters running through the flats to escape being caught.

Eileen Collins

My family was always Republican and we did not recognise the British Government as our liberators. If you look at any photographs of that time in August 1969 when the army came onto the streets, every gun is pointed in towards the Bogside, not away from the Bogside. I remember everybody was over the moon. I thought, they're not in here to protect us, they're here to protect the interests of the business people. We kept the police out. I was a married woman and I was willing to go out and fight with petrol bombs.

The previous night a lot of buildings went up in flames and the police were beat to the ropes. They were glad to see the army coming in because they were exhausted. I remember me and my mother going down to William Street for

Martin McGuinness and Christopher McKnight observe British troops searching the lifts in the flats on a raid in the early 1980s.

Mural of Stephen McConomy who was only 11 when he was killed by a plastic bullet fired by the army in the shadow of the flats on Fahan Street in April 1982.

something to eat. Big Vinny Coyle, Eddie McAteer and the rest of them were in Rossville Street. The news had already come through that the army were coming in. I remember looking at them all and saying to myself, God, what a day, to see the British Army in Derry. Everybody was clapping and cheering, and my mother looked at me and we put our eyes up to heaven. We knew it wasn't going to last.

They came in with their sandbags around the bottom of Rossville Street. This was their way of 'protecting' us. Anyone with a brain would have known they were only there to protect the interests of the business people. I remember my mother went down with a bread knife and slashed the sandbags. She said it was her way of welcoming them into her country. I thought it significant that the Brit thought my mother was coming down with a cup of tea. Instead, she was coming down to let him know that she considered him her enemy. People would have scorned her and said she was an oul' rebel. I was very proud of her that particular night.

Eventually, attitudes changed when the people started getting harassed. A couple of fellas were beaten up by drunken British soldiers in the town. Then in the summer of 1971 Desmond Beattie, Seamus Cusack and Hugh Herron were shot by the army. It was around then that people started to really see that British soldiers weren't their protectors. Then Bloody Sunday happened which changed everything.

In mid-1972, there were rumours going around that the army were going to take over the flats. We thought it couldn't happen. But then we heard the helicopters, they were going all night long. Whatever it was they were putting on the roofs, probably the reinforced observation posts at each end, they brought them in by helicopter. There wasn't much we could do to British soldiers with guns. We just had to accept it.

There was a lot of security, front and back of the flats. When they changed guard, the young fellas threw stones at them or threw things out the windows. The Brits had to change their times because the young fellas used to have everything ready from the flats to fire down at them. I remember there was a scuffle with the young fellas once and one of the soldiers let the gun off and there was a gaping hole in the tiles in the front of the lifts where the bullet went through. We just ignored the Brits.

They used to send the younger ones down to the shops for lemonade and fags. My son was about seven or eight. I had warned him not to go messages for the Brits. He came in complaining all the others were getting money for going to the shops and he wasn't. I said, 'Aye, you stone them and you'll get money.' He came in five minutes later and said, 'Mammy, I didn't go any messages. I stoned them, and they still didn't give me any money.' I had the youngster afraid to go near them because they had guns. You didn't know if the IRA were going to open up, so I was safeguarding the children.

You knew the army were watching you all the time they were on the roof. The flats were shaped like a 'U' and they were positioned at one end and at each corner of the flats. Most of the bedrooms looked out the back into the square and because they had nightlights you were always aware that they were there. You always kept your bedroom curtains closed because they could see everything from where they were positioned. If they were changing guard when you were putting the children out to school, you were always afraid something was going to start and maybe a child was going to get hurt. The lifts of the flats always seemed to be broken when they were there. I think they were sabotaged deliberately by the Brits because they were afraid of gunmen going up on the roof. It meant that young mothers with children had to carry the prams up themselves.

The stairs from the fifth to the eighth floor were sealed off to protect the British soldiers. Rubbish was thrown down chutes into skips in the middle of the flats beside the lifts. The Brits had no facilities. They must have thrown their rubbish and their toilet waste down the chutes. These were only emptied once a week and there was always a foul smell, especially in the good weather.

The IRA shot two soldiers dead in the flats in November 1973. So you were always aware of the possible danger from attacks. But the IRA tried not to risk the residents being caught up in things.

The army observation post on the top of the Embassy building overlooking the Bogside.

Billy Carlin

The army were dug in at the top of the flats when we moved in. I remember one night in particular, my father, myself and Kevin were coming back from my sister's house and we were in the lift when we heard shots. When we got to the top floor two soldiers were lying there. I think one of them was dead and the other was severely injured. It was a sight that I wouldn't like to see too often. Another soldier came running down from the sangar up the stairs and he was in pure panic. My father disarmed him because he would have shot somebody that night. I'm sure of it. Within minutes the whole place was saturated with soldiers and you could hear the noise of the Saracens down below. The next thing, all the windows in the flats were open and everybody was throwing out bottles and all sorts at them.

For a while after that they stopped the lifts going up to the eighth floor. We lived on the Rossville Street side so we had to get out of the lift at the fifth floor and walk across to get up the back stairs to our floor. You couldn't come out of the lift straight onto the stairs, they had it all blocked off at that time.

When any rioting started around the flats I joined in but only got involved for five or ten minutes. My parents were very strict and they used to come down and just lift me out of it which was very embarrassing. Everybody else was running away from the snatch squads and I was trying to run away from my ma. I would rather get caught by the Brits. That's the way it always was for us. When the soldiers were living in the flats they used to give me a hard time. This went on for ages and it got to the stage where I didn't use the lifts anymore because of the abuse.

Philomena Wilson

The problems began when the army moved in. They were the cause of the dampness and stopping the lifts from working. Because of the army, the flats gradually became a place that wasn't very pleasant to live in. I always felt that their eyes were on you

and your children, watching you all the time. No matter what time I came in at night I felt that they were either taking my photograph or watching me. Before the army ever entered the flats I never had a problem, I felt very secure, I could have come in from work at two in the morning and I didn't have a problem. But when the army came I didn't like it.

People resented the army in the flats because they battered every doorway in and broke every light and I thought to myself, this is going to be 1969 all over again when we lived in the Wells and my father and mother had to barricade themselves in against the B-Specials when the police beat the doors in. I thought the army was going to do something the same that night when they first moved in.

At that time I had moved into the second floor and sometimes when we went up to the eighth floor to visit my neighbours we got a lot of aggro from the army. They never had any respect for us so I would have no respect for them. Their language was appalling to me.

It was a prison when the army moved into the flats, without a doubt. No matter where you went they were there, even when I came in from work at night they were sitting at the chute. It spoiled it for me and it spoiled it for quite a few other people, they just took the place over completely.

The RUC raided me about three times. I had a lot of friends visiting and the only way they would have known that was through the army in the flats. But it was worse when they came in to do a big raid of the flats with the CS gas. They didn't just fire one round, it was steady one after another and it seeped in through every flat.

We had to dampen cloths to put over our mouths to help us breathe, even the children did it. I am very asthmatic and to this day I blame the CS gas for it.

Terry Lamberton

The British Army became part of everybody's lives when growing up in the 1970s. There were riots every Saturday on Rossville Street or William Street. Children used the staircase of the Rossville Street block to get the best view of the rioting through the vertical planks. They were waiting to see the crowds running back up Rossville Street when the army made a snatch. Someone once said it was like the Saturday matinee.

For some reason the army often used to park an armoured Saracen on Rossville Street, just at the entrance into the car park. Pilot's Row wasn't built at the time and it was all just waste ground, so you could just go around the Saracen. The youngsters threw stones, bottles and anything they could get at them. The soldiers rarely caught anyone because when the rioters saw the back doors of the Saracen opening, they ran into the flats and straight up the steps to hide until it was safe to come back down again.

I recall sitting in the living room of our flat one night with my family. My uncle had come in with a broken clock to see if he could get it fixed. Suddenly shooting started and everyone dived to the floor. It was very loud and continuous so we all crawled into the bathroom. When the shooting stopped, we stayed in the bathroom until we could hear movement on the balcony. My father and uncle went down to see what was going on. We then heard the roar of English accents ordering everybody out of their flats so we all went down to the balcony.

All the men were lined up against the railings and one soldier was going up and down shouting, 'Shoot them all and we will get the gunmen.' My older brother had just come back from a football match in Bull Park and was stuck at the bottom of the stairway. The army had blocked it off and weren't allowing anybody up. My mother was arguing with the officer to let someone down to get him. A man approached my mother and the officer and said he would go and get him. The officer eventually gave in and let him go. We found out years later that the man was one of the gunmen.

My mother then remembered my granny who was sick in her bed in her flat on a lower level. She went down to see her, but some soldiers refused her access. She went back up to the officer and started complaining about my granny being left on her own when she was sick. So the officer agreed to let my uncle go down to stay with her. The funny thing about it was, as my uncle left to go down to my granny's all the other men on the balcony were getting searched. So if my uncle had been searched, they would have found the clock in his coat and would have thought he was making a bomb.

Martha McClelland
I moved into the flats on the day of Patsy O'Hara's funeral. I don't think people realised at the time, but looking back, it was a worldwide centre of resistance.

People did things every day to make sure that people like Margaret Thatcher were not going to get away with killing people. We were going to stand up for our community. People didn't realise how important what we were doing was. We were putting all our energies towards it. We didn't realise how significant it was on the world scale. It was a very sad, very horrific time, but at the same time it was what you were doing for survival. You could either sit down and take it or you could band together and fight for survival. That's what we were doing. People didn't realise how historical it was and how important it was. A lot of that centred around the flats. They were a symbol and a very important symbol.

Charlie McMenamin
As the years went on, and the Troubles got worse, a lot of people were affected. Hugh Gilmour, who died on Bloody Sunday, was living in the flats at the time, and we knew all the people who died.

A lot of the younger people were involved in the rioting in 1968 and 1969, and a lot of people got involved in politics through all the campaigning that went on in the flats. It was the University of Freedom. There's a lot of history there.

Anonymous soldier, extract from Brits Speak Out *publication*
There was an Observation Post (OP) on top of the Rossville Flats, overlooking the Bogside. I only manned it once, for a week, with two others. The floor was armour-plated and bomb-proofed. There were various steel doors that you had to go through to get in, and then a cage door like a prison. It took time to bring in supplies as one solider would have to be on the roof, one at the bottom of the stairs waiting to open the cage door, and another one would be at the top of the stairs. At night you would sometimes hear people shouting and banging the gate, but you knew that there was no chance of them getting in. The toilet was a Portaloo on top of the roof. It was a strange feeling, and funny, to think that you were doing what you were in full sight of the city. The OP was closed after the first year of us being there. I don't think that it was doing much good as everyone knew it was there, so if people were going to do a hijacking or whatever, they would make sure that they were out of view.

Governor Walker's monument on the city Walls overlooked the flats until it was blown
up by the IRA in 1973.

Youths gather at the top entrance to the flats on Fahan Street
to confront the security forces on the Walls.

This page and following: The area around the flats witnessed ongoing attacks on the police and army over many years which caused much damage and resulted in widespread disruption to people and traffic.

Crowds gather for a protest meeting at Free Derry Corner, circa mid-1980s.

Housing Protests

Although the residents were initially happy with their new accommodation, it soon became obvious to them that the living conditions were quite shoddy and even a potential health hazard due to the amount of asbestos in the walls.

On 1 July 1968 the Housing Trust (HT) announced that rents were to be increased for all its housing units by between 20% and 25%, taking effect on 30 September 1968. After a vigorous campaign of resistance led by the newly formed Rossville Flats tenants' association – mentored by the Derry Housing Action Committee (DHAC) and notable activists such as Dermie McClenaghan, Eamon Melaugh, Eamonn McCann and Fionnbarra Ó Dochartaig – the HT announced in late July that their rent rebate scheme would be extended to virtually all tenants. It was a notable early success for the collective campaign by tenants from across the area against rent increases.

The Rossville Flats tenants' association became the focal point for the residents from the mid-1970s onwards to express their anger and discontent to the bureaucrats about the deterioration of their living conditions, most notably the all-pervading dampness. Politicians from the wider Nationalist community added their support and organisational skills to the efforts of the residents to get the flats demolished and more suitable traditional housing provided. Eventually their combined efforts proved successful.

Martin McGuinness looks over the damp conditions in one of the flats.

Eileen Collins

The roof started to leak with the abuse it was getting when the Brits moved in. The insulation between the walls left the flats very damp. I remember the water coming in. I could hear the rats at night, so we moved the children into the big bedroom, which was ours originally. It was the warmest and we moved into the living room to sleep.

When the flats were being tumbled, most of the asbestos in the partition walls had been eaten away by the rats. People were not aware then how dangerous asbestos was. The only wall that was concrete was the outer wall, but the rest was just a fine sheet of plywood. If there had have been a big fire in those flats a lot of people would have been killed. The electrical wires weren't very good. Plus, you had the gas heating danger.

The flats were home to people who never really had anything. But the way it was in Derry, you asked for little and got even less. People didn't realise what they were entitled to, like play facilities and other things. It wasn't until the civil rights movement that people started to rise up and look for things. The flats by that stage

Rita Moore lifts her damp carpets
in 74 Donagh Place.

Martin McGuinness and Barney McFadden
help residents move out of their damp flats.

Mary McSheffrey (née McGilloway, left) reveals the amount of dampness she was
enduring in 75 Donagh Place and a young neighbour shares her plight.

An unhappy resident in 32 Donagh Place examines the dampness in her outside wall.

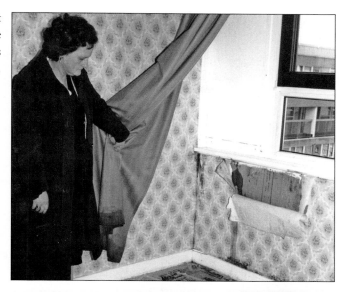

Margaret Quigg demonstrates the level of dampness in 17 Donagh Place.

Below: Seamus Keenan and Mitchel McLaughlin advised residents on resolving their housing problems.

were starting to deteriorate. Although most people were glad to be there originally, it was obvious to me they were just built as a kind of a 'get the people housed quick' approach. The structure of the buildings seemed to be thrown up like a pack of cards.

Celine Carlin

The Housing Executive let them deteriorate. They let them off to single people who were abusing them. They became dilapidated to an extent. When we moved in there was nobody on the eighth floor at Donagh Place. In the middle block, where we lived originally, there was only us and Alan Fox's mother, Kitty. Kitty lived two doors above me because she had a walk-in one-bedroom flat.

I think they should have been refurbished and brought up to date. Maybe not everybody wanted to live in them, but I was quite happy. My wains loved them. The neighbours took turns to keep the place clean. You did your landing every weekend. If we had bleach or Jeyes Fluid we scrubbed down the back and front stairs. We did the bin chutes on the eighth floor ourselves.

The way I look at it, some people felt that it was okay to knock them down. But I didn't feel like that. Outsiders from other areas started hanging around them and that's how they became dilapidated. It wasn't the people who lived in them.

Boarded-up flats on the fifth floor, Mura Place.

A workman measures up to board off one of the derelict flats.

Gary Meenan observes the dampness in 31 Donagh Place.

Kitty Kirk examines her drenched carpets in 36 Donagh Place.

Martha McClelland

I was part of the tenants' committee along with Jean Friel and Joan Doherty and a lot of others. We were campaigning and organising petitions and working with Sinn Féin to get the flats knocked down because of the constant problems and the design faults.

At one stage there was a major fire in the stairs. It knocked out all of our electricity for weeks. People were getting their food and stuff cooked and prepared over at Pilot's Row. I was quite involved in that as well.

The protests in 1983-84 were up at the Housing Executive offices. That's when there was a lot of flooding and things. We had protests for the media at Waterloo Place and at the flats when the fire took place. Derry didn't have any central government buildings to have a protest in front of. You couldn't go up to the seat of government, you could go to the Strand Road, but it wasn't quite the same.

Billy Carlin

My mother was involved in the tenants' association and at the start of the campaign in 1978 she would have been up with the placards along with John Tierney and Jimmy McFadden in Bishop Street where the Housing Executive offices were at the time. Thomas Craig, a wee man with glasses, was the first Protestant/Unionist mayor to come into the Bogside about a housing problem. He came into our flat because that's where they were having the discussions. There was a big hullabaloo being made of it at the time, it was just unheard of.

Thomas Craig, Unionist mayor of Derry, on the eighth floor of the flats with
Ann Ryan and her daughter Melissa in 1979.

Everybody knew everybody's business because the walls were that thin you could hear people moving about two flats down the walkway. You could break though into the next flat very easy, there was only a door and an asbestos sheet between them. I think it was some kind of in-built safety feature. If there was a fire you were supposed to break through into the adjoining flat and then you could get into the next one if you needed to and so on. That was their justification for safety. They were only egg boxes at the end of the day, with a bit of concrete around the outside holding the structure together.

The stench of urine in the lifts was unbelievable at times. It was awful. You had to hold your breath getting from the ground floor to the top. And then when you went into the chute area to throw your rubbish down it used to be awful, too; it used to knock me sick. The caretaker's heart was broken trying to keep it clean for everybody. But what scared me most was when we went up the back stairs, the glass had been kicked out of the side walls and there were big gaps there. How nobody fell out I'll never know. It wouldn't be allowed nowadays.

When you were young, you didn't think much about why they wanted the flats demolished. As you got older you could see they weren't a good place for young families to rear their kids. They would have been ideal for student accommodation or maybe pensioners, providing the lifts were working. They wouldn't get away with building them today, even just in terms of health and safety.

Martin Dunleavy

One particular morning me and my da had to get up at five o'clock. A certain person had sat in a sink in an empty flat and the sink had come away from the wall. It was seriously flooding the flat below it and there was somebody living in there. My da went up to the top floor to knock off the water on the roof and I started hammering in the pipes that were burst. He was shouting down to me, 'I'll knock the water on.' I shouted up, 'Aye.' So, he knocked the water on. But I hadn't the pipes hammered in right so at five o'clock in the morning I was standing up to my neck in water, soaked.

They wouldn't even give us a place to operate from. We had a bin store that my da used as an 'office' for 15 years until he eventually got somewhere to work from. It was an old flat. We had two actually. We had one which ended up getting wrecked, so we moved out of that into another one. It eventually got wrecked as well.

People threw everything out down the chutes. Toilet seats were the worst because they'd block the chutes, nothing got past a toilet seat. We had to use a big 84lb weight to free the chutes. We pounded on the chute until it moved. My da nearly broke his back with that weight. If the lift was broken, we used to cart it the whole way from the bottom to the top. Sometimes the chute gave way before

Rossville residents take their campaign to the Guildhall. Includes Dickie Valley, Bridie O'Brien, Mary Friel, Cathy Dalzell, Deirdre Hannaway and John Tierney.

the rubbish moved. We broke more chutes than enough. In fact, one nearly killed people because the side of the chute flew out up at Fahan Street.

We were knee-deep in asbestos dust at times after the army raids and nobody thought about getting us a health check. The army didn't care. They kicked through anything, asbestos panels and everything, and as usual we were left to clear it up. Little did they know, at that time, they were damaging their own health as well by busting it all up.

John Tierney

The rehousing and demolition of the Rossville Flats came about when individual residents started going to the Housing Executive (HE) to complain about their own homes. It was only when they started talking to each other they realised it was not just their flat that was damp but a lot of them. It was then that they decided to all go together to protest at the HE and Council meetings in the Guildhall for the demolition of the flats. It wasn't just the dampness that they were complaining about – it was the way they would have to carry their groceries or children or prams to the top floor when the lifts were out of order for weeks on end. And there were times when coffins had to be carried down the stairs when the lifts weren't working.

Not too long after the protests had started, the lifts were out of order again which ended up to our advantage. Someone had been sick and the doctor was sent for. But when he arrived and saw that he had to walk up the stairs to see the patient

Housing Executive Board members observe progress on the construction of the new roofs on the flats designed to help alleviate the dampness in 1983.

Nancy Meenan, Gary Meenan, John McDevitt, Shelia McCann, John Shiels, Ginny Gallagher, Jim Collins and Terry Lamberton join the protests.

Above: Yvonne McKnight, Shelia McCann, Moira Carr, Kathleen McGrellis, Margaret Quigg, Gary Meenan, Rita Moore, Rosemary McKinney, Rose McGrory and friends at the HE offices on Bishop Street.

Below: Protesting about plans to build the Pilot's Row Centre instead of much-needed houses in the area. Includes: Evelyn Valley, Joan Doherty, Bernie Tierney, Ann Ryan, Mary Lamberton, Bernie Goode, Bridie Ferguson, Betty Kirk, Cathy Doherty and Dickie Valley.

Martin McGuinness joins residents on their protest at Bishop Street.

he refused. Dr Raymond McClean was our councillor at the time so we got him to get all the doctors in the city to sign a petition to get the flats demolished.

It was the Unionist mayor who got us front-page publicity when he visited the flats at our request and said that he would not keep pigs in them.

As the campaign progressed, we were told that John O'Gorman, the HE Chief Executive, was coming with other board members to visit the flats to see for themselves what kind of conditions we were living in. After the visit we were told it would be too expensive to demolish them and rehouse everyone. They decided instead to spend £1.5 million on a new roof and new windows around 1983 to try to solve the dampness problem. The residents and Council told them they would be throwing good money away.

After all the work was done it became clear that none of the problems had been fixed. After this, we knew we would have to keep up the pressure on the HE and Council if we wanted the flats demolished and the residents rehoused. We had further meetings with the HE board in Belfast and with British ministers. On one occasion a minister actually came down to view the flats.

Many of the flats became so bad with dampness that, in the end, the HE said they were unliveable and had to be boarded up. This was a victory for us, but it created another problem when the young ones pulled the boards off the flats and started using them as drinking dens. This always annoyed whatever residents still occupied the adjacent flats. The residents had no choice but to keep the campaign going until eventually the HE agreed to knock them down over a three-year timeframe.

Flats Demolished and Memories Made

After many years of lobbying, street protests and pickets, and a sustained publicity drive, the Housing Executive sought permission from the NI Office to order the demolition of block one of the flats facing onto Rossville Street in 1985. The HE wished to retain the other two blocks for questionable reasons but this was resisted and in the end they agreed to tumble them all. Block one came down in 1986 and the remaining blocks fell in 1989. The residents found either private accommodation or social housing across the city with some even being rehoused in the footprint of the flats themselves in Joseph Place.

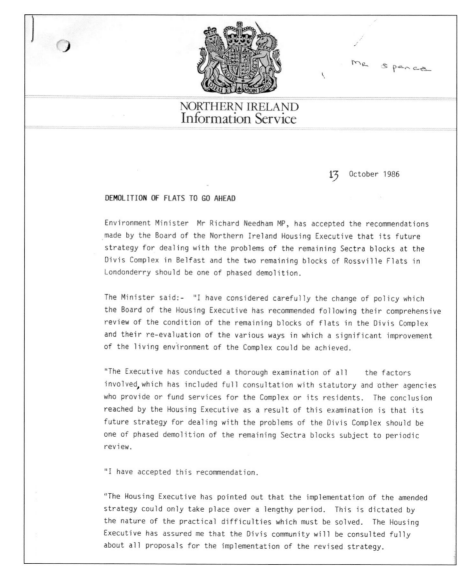

MR Spence

NORTHERN IRELAND
Information Service

13   October 1986

DEMOLITION OF FLATS TO GO AHEAD

Environment Minister Mr Richard Needham MP, has accepted the recommendations made by the Board of the Northern Ireland Housing Executive that its future strategy for dealing with the problems of the remaining Sectra blocks at the Divis Complex in Belfast and the two remaining blocks of Rossville Flats in Londonderry should be one of phased demolition.

The Minister said:- "I have considered carefully the change of policy which the Board of the Housing Executive has recommended following their comprehensive review of the condition of the remaining blocks of flats in the Divis Complex and their re-evaluation of the various ways in which a significant improvement of the living environment of the Complex could be achieved.

"The Executive has conducted a thorough examination of all   the factors involved, which has included full consultation with statutory and other agencies who provide or fund services for the Complex or its residents. The conclusion reached by the Housing Executive as a result of this examination is that its future strategy for dealing with the problems of the Divis Complex should be one of phased demolition of the remaining Sectra blocks subject to periodic review.

"I have accepted this recommendation.

"The Housing Executive has pointed out that the implementation of the amended strategy could only take place over a lengthy period. This is dictated by the nature of the practical difficulties which must be solved. The Housing Executive has assured me that the Divis community will be consulted fully about all proposals for the implementation of the revised strategy.

So after 23 years of dominating the Bogside and Derry skyline, the ill-fated experiment in public authority high-rise living, designed and planned with a concealed agenda, was proven to be a failure. Over that time the flats housed hundreds of families, many of whom spent their formative years there, sharing good times and bad. It is probably true to say their feeling and emotions are mixed about their experiences in the Rossville Flats. But most would harbour fond memories of the community spirit and interaction that forged lasting friendships with neighbours old and new that carried on to other estates, roads and streets across the area.

John Tierney
Eventually, the HE decided to knock down the first block on Rossville Street but keep the other two blocks. They said this was because they wanted to keep the shops under block two to service the community. The residents were totally against this and they had the support of the shop owners who themselves wanted all the flats demolished. So the HE then said they would knock down blocks one and two but keep the ones on Fahan Street. But the Fahan Street residents felt even more disadvantaged as every time there was a Loyalist march in the town they would end up getting abuse and their windows smashed from the gangs of marchers on the Walls.

So the HE had no choice but to knock them all down. As a result of the demolition order, all the residents of the flats went on to the priority housing list for new houses in the area. At that time the housing list was very long in the city and we could understand that it was hard for people who had already been waiting a long time to be housed to see the Rossville residents getting rehoused before them. But overall I think we had the support of the whole town in getting the flats demolished.

I have to give full credit to the residents of the flats, they were the ones who protested for ages and declared they were not putting up with it anymore, they were the ones who got the flats demolished in the end.

In saying that, if you talk to any of those people now most would say they miss them. And if you dig deep into what it is they really miss it is the friendships they had there. They miss sitting out on the balcony until two or three in the morning. They miss the good community relations in them. They always seem to forget the bad conditions we all lived in but in all reality could not have endured much longer. It is nice to remember the good times with the good neighbours we had and I think that's what we all miss most about living in the Rossville Flats.

Eileen Collins
Overall, I felt nostalgic about my time in the flats. As time went on, people started to agitate to get them demolished. But I left and bought a house in the town because the Housing Executive was going to house us out in Galliagh or beyond which did not suit me. That's where a lot of my neighbours ended up.

Children play as the flats are demolished all around them.

But some of them refused to move and campaigned until they were allocated housing where they wanted to be. So they had to build a lot more houses to facilitate them. That's how Ballymagroarty sprouted up. It was the closest to the centre of the town, apart from Creggan and Creggan was already full. The old houses in the Bog have now been refurbished and people are paying vast amounts of money to get staying there.

There were a lot of people who lived in the flats who joined the IRA after Bloody Sunday and some of them are up in the graveyard now. It is very sad when you think about some of the tragic things that happened. But life goes on.

Sheila Brown
In a way I was sorry I left the flats, but we had to close up the hairdressing shop because every Saturday the stones were flying and nobody would come out. We had good neighbours, good people, down in the shops and we had good neighbours in the houses on the other side as well, but it was one of those things.

I don't really remember them being taken down. When I saw they were gone I thought it was terrible. I suppose it is just the price you have to pay for progress. But I thought to myself, wouldn't it be great for any young man or woman who wasn't married that could now be doing with a wee place. But then the other new houses wouldn't be there and a lot of people have been relocated, with good houses put there in their place. It was another time and another life, but I can say I was happy enough living there.

Martha McClelland
When the flats were being demolished they were vandalised. Cookers and radios and everything were thrown out the windows so that the flats were left empty and open. This meant that the British soldiers couldn't hide and shoot people using the flats as cover. At that time, people were being moved out of the flats and British troops were being moved in, undercover, at night, and staying there sometimes for up to a week, putting people in the flats and in the Bog under observation. At one stage there were shots fired from the flats and it wasn't the IRA who were shooting. People from outside Derry did not realise that this was why some of the flats facing Rossville Street were semi-derelict. I think they were taken down because they were too much of a reminder of the Battle of the Bogside, too much of a reminder that the Brits were entering our territory and that the Crown didn't rule here.

I was rehoused in the summer of 1987 and I missed the camaraderie of my neighbours. I miss the friendships and being right in the city centre. I don't miss the dirty stairwells or anything, and I'm lucky enough to have a garden now, but I really miss the people, great neighbours.

Billy Carlin

I left the flats in 1980 when I got married. They were finished at that stage. They built new houses for the residents up around Little Diamond and William Street, it was the start of the end for the flats really. I was living in Victoria Park at the time the flats were demolished so it did not really affect me. It would have been different if I had been still visiting the flats on a daily basis to see my mother and father, but they weren't there then.

When they started knocking them down I remember looking at old photographs and saying, that was where I lived in Rossville Street. I could point out the flat, it was the third window from the left, and the third window down from the top, and that was our living room and our kitchen area. There are times now when I am passing the place I just see houses there and I think, I used to live there, pointing to the sky.

They served a purpose, I suppose, at that time. Housing in Derry was pretty poor and they had to do something. I don't know if they meant it to be a long-term solution. I don't think they should have been going as long as they were, but for a stopgap at the time it was fantastic.

Martin Dunleavy

In 1987 we were offered a house in Creggan Street. There was some difference when we left. In Creggan Street we had a small back garden and a big massive back yard for the first time. I found it hard to get used to looking out and seeing people passing up and down the street, right outside your front door or window. I never knew that in the Rossville Flats. It took a while to get used to.

My mother didn't really like living in the flats to be quite honest. She was really pleased when she got the move. I don't think she would ever go back to Rossville Street, never mind the flats.

For me, it was sad. There was a part of me was glad to leave. I had some very unusual experiences in the flats, especially when I worked in them. My whole life revolved around them. Working in them, I was there 24 hours a day. Very rarely was I away from them.

Philomena Wilson

I was very sorry when they knocked the flats down. I think if they had been refurbished properly they could be still there for the people. But I did not want to live there anymore, I wanted away so I left before they were tumbled.

I was on holidays and when I came back, Ann Ryan told me we had both been housed in William Street. When I first moved to William Street – this is very hard to believe – I didn't like it because I had a front door and a back door and I didn't feel really safe. I felt more secure when I was over there before any bother started, before the army and the police moved in. It took me a long time to get used to William Street because when I was in the flats, I always felt fairly safe walking home at all hours. But it is better now, and some of our neighbours are around the corner now – Marie Johnson, Celine Carlin, the Ryans, John Tierney. If those flats could talk…

Annette Harkin

They were the best days of my life. When we moved from the flats to William Street it broke my mother's heart. Life was easy in the flats, and everybody was like your family. I live in a house now and I have three children of my own, but if the flats were up and running I would happily move back.

You knew everybody and everybody knew you. You could be in one flat for your lunch and another for your dinner. It was a great place to live, the best in the world.

Deirdre Conaghan

I had my two sons when I lived in the flats and I'm nearly sure I was the last to move out. We left just before they were knocked down. I moved to Corporation Street then. It was very sad to leave because we had brilliant craic and when the riots were going on there was always something to watch. We were just around the corner from the Rocking Chair bar which would have been my local then.

It was very quiet towards the end, it was getting eerie. Everybody that left just fired everything over the balcony into the back square. It was sad leaving, it was the end of an era and the end of the flats. I had been there since I was 17 and we left in 1988.

I would love to go back to the flats if they were still there. It was the place to be. It was a good community and there were always parties and community events and you had a bird's-eye view of the riots.

Carn Rossville

By Marta Mhic Giolla Aolain

A roar and such shaking and
No means of escape
I snatched up the cat and
Ran through to the bedroom window
Through settling dust
Block three of Rossville Flats
My home
Folded down on top of itself
Amputated
Mortality heaped between my home
And Pilot's Row Centre

Grey dust choked me
As I saw the woman
Who passed my window at nine
Return
Bulging plastic Wellworths' bags
Lengthening each arm,
She passed the folded flats
Including that one on the fifth floor
Her home for 19 years
Balconies
The veins and arteries of the flats
Pulsating
With children and tricycles
Their laughter and rage
That balcony outside her door
Crumbled concrete now
A mouthful of gravel
Spewed from the jaws of the digger
To litter the tarmac for seven days

The Ballad of Rossville Flats

Well, in the sweet old town of Derry, 'neath the ancient city Walls
On the site where a cattle market used to be
Well, they built a concrete monster back then as I recall
In the heady days of 1963
Well, those steel and concrete cages, they stacked up row on row
The architects they treated us with scorn
Then they filled them up with people with nowhere else to go
And the legend of the Rossville Flats was born

So all you gentle people who lived in Garvan Place
In Mura and in Donagh, at last you've won your case
I'm sure you all remember, as I remember yet
That our days in Rossville Flats, we won't forget
Well, the tall blocks they were standing, 80 feet or more
And they stood on three sides of the market square
On the face of our dear city, they were a running sore
As they fell into a state of disrepair
Well, they had their share of fire, they had their share of flood
They had their share of poverty and pain
And their hope lived through the battles, through bitterness and blood
And the hope of finding peace was all in vain

Well, the flats soon found their picture hanging in the hall of fame
They were held aloft for all the world to see
There was not a single person who hadn't heard their name
And now they're part of Irish history
One day as I looked over the burnt and ugly smell
The wretched sight, it left me feeling numb
For life in there for people was just a living hell
An ill-conceived and soul-destroying slum

Then in the summer of '89, we lifted up our eyes
And watched as the monster crumbled to the ground
As 10,000 tons of concrete descended from the skies
The roar of thunder was the only sound
Yet it filled some hearts with sadness to finally see the end
And we heaved a sigh as the dust and the rubble fell
Then we raised our hats together as to a poor departed friend
And to the dear old Rossville Flats we bid farewell

Rossville Flats Tenants – 1966 to 1989

Hundreds of families lived in the Rossville Flats between their first occupancy in 1966 until their demolition in 1989. Below is a list of tenants, taken from the electoral register, who officially occupied each flat in chronological order. In later years, the lack of social housing in Derry meant that some people were forced to squat in the flats so they were never formally acknowledged in the tenancy records.

Garvan Place

1. McGuinness/Henderson
2. Swarth/McConomy/McCarron
3. Cunningham/Maguire
4. Bridge/Meenan
5. Dunleavy/Johnson
6. Gallagher/Lynch/Canning/ Connor
7. Doherty
8. McDermott/McDermott & Gallagher/O'Hagan/McKinney
9. Doherty/Bonney/Gillespie
10. Henderson/Kennedy/Birtles
11. Dunleavy/McCafferty/McCarron/ McNoone
12. McCrudden/Casey
13. Murray/McLaughlin/Doherty
14. Sheils/Rodden
15. Morris/Roddy/McDaid
16. Kelly/Wilson
17. Nash/Quigley/Rooney
18. Patterson/Gilmore/Collins
19. Friel/O'Hagan/McConnell
20. Collins/Kelly
21. Doherty/McShane/McConnell/ McGinley/Devine
22. O'Reilly/Conaghan/McGinley
23. Gilmore/McConomy/ McKeever/Strain
24. McLaughlin/Hillen/Patton
25. Kineton/Carlin/Magill/ McClelland
26. Ryan/Coyle/Deehan/Harkin
27. McLaughlin/Carlin/Doherty
28. Nelis/McDaid/Ryan/Devine
29. Bonner/Meehan/Ryan
30. Doherty/McConnell
31. Tucker/Kelly/Deery/Meenan & Harkin
32. Smith/Cassidy/McClintock/ McIntyre/Doherty
33. Watts/O'Hagan/O'Connell/ McLaughlin/Conaghan
34. Logue/Bonner/Healy/Sheils & Donnelly
35. Connolly/Ogle/Green/ Lawrence
36. McGowan/McShane/Doherty
37. Housing Trust/Rossville Flats Community Centre

Mura Place

1. Dalton/Strain
2. Pyne/Gorman/McBride
3. Sheerin/Jones/Harkin
4. Sheerin/Flanagan/Glen/O'Neill/ Duddy/Graham
5. Moore/Moore
6. Long/Scarlett/O'Brien
7. Higgins
8. Unwin/McCafferty/Lynch/ Robinson

9. McClintock
10. Moore/Moore/Harkin/Fox/O'Neill
11. Ward
12. Curran/Goode/McCafferty/Friel/ Jackson/Doherty
13. McCafferty/Green/Barr/McDaid
14. Donaghey
15. Kavanagh/Farrell/Gallagher/ Dunleavy/Friel/Conaghan
16. McDowell/Birtles/McConnell
17. Gallagher/Campbell/Doherty/ Scarlett
18. Doherty/McCauley/McCauley & McIntyre
19. McAnea/Jones
20. McLaughlin/Norris/Tierney/ O'Donnell
21. Harkin
22. McGilloway/Barr/Long/Butterfield
23. Ramsey/Hannaway
24. O'Neill/Moore/Lindsay/Deeney
25. O'Connor/Coyle
26. Faulkner/Hannaway/Devine
27. Turner/McLaughlin
28. McDermott/Begley/Doherty
29. Horner/Casey/Murray/Hegarty/ Donnelly/Boyle/McGee
30. Brown/Johnston/Gallagher
31. Wood/McCarron
32. O'Neill
33. Hutton/Brown
34. McGinnes/O'Donnell/Deery/ McCarron/Henry/Gorman
35. Boyle
36. Norris/Rouse
37. Tyre/Fox/McCann
38. Morrison/Green/Radcliffe/ Dauncey
39. Cairns/Hamilton/Gallen/ Donaghey
40. McCallion/Lynch/Robinson/ Conaghan/Bonner
41. Sheerin/Bonner/Quigley/ McFarland/Glenn/Bonner/ Dunleavy
42. McCarron/Roddy
43. Glenn/Morrison/O'Hagan/Mallett
44. Cassidy/McClelland/Warren/ McCarron
45. Carlin/Sheehan/Seacon/Friel
46. Harkin/McNulty/Etman/Wruck/ Kelly/Doherty
47. Rouse
48. Doherty
49. Johnstone/McCarron/Quigley/ McConnell
50. McCauley/Diamond
51. Divin/O'Neill
52. Eaton/McLaughlin/Coyle/ O'Hagan
53. Harkin/Gallagher/Anderson
54. McCauley/Hegarty/Kalkman & Hegarty
55. McCarron/O'Reilly/McGarrigle/ Valley & McCauley/Birtles
56. Diamond/McCourt/Ryan/ McLaughlin/Hegarty
57. Ball/O'Donnell
58. Nash/Gallagher/Goode/Barlow & Smith
59. Crawley
60. Chambers/Hogan/Forbes/Moore
61. Hegarty/Moore/McCay/Ramsey/ Mackie
62. Meehan
63. O'Hara/Henry/Kineton
64. Duffy/Donaghey
65. Barr/Conaghan
66. Shiels/Ryan
67. Casey/Barlow/Palmer

Donagh Place

1. McCauley/Moore/Tierney/Doherty
2. Doherty/Mullan/McNoone/Rodden
3. McIntyre/Havlin/Donohoe/Leggett
4. Doherty/Smith/McCourt/Murphy/Duddy/Harkin
5. McLaughlin/Gallagher/Campbell
6. McFadden
7. McGahey/Valley/Harkin
8. O'Neill/Carlin/Doherty
9. McGilloway/Friel
10. Hegarty/White/McCrossan/McNoone/Campbell
11. Kyle/Roddy
12. Kennedy/Tierney/Stevenson
13. Doherty
14. Doherty/Roddy/Quigley/Shiels/Toland
15. McKnight
16. Cunningham/Noone/Duffy
17. Doherty/Doherty/McMahon/Bonner/Quigg
18. McFadden/Millar/Earnshaw
19. Gargaro/Deery
20. McGrory/Doherty/Farren/O'Neill/Quigg
21. McGuinness/Meenan
22. Mooney/Ó Comáin
23. McCann/Rodgers
24. Meenan
25. Wade/Casey/McLaughlin
26. Fox/Gilmore/McGrory/Campbell
27. Stewart/Donnelly/Kelly
28. McGavigan/Green/O'Kane/Fitzpatrick/Hannaway/McFadden
29. Irwin/McGavigan/Rodgers
30. Carlin/McNulty/McCluskey/Rudd
31. Boyle/Meenan/Roddy
32. McConomy/Ryan/McElhinney
33. O'Kane/McGovern/Dunbar
34. McGowan
35. Fox/Billington/Gallagher
36. Higgins/Bonney/Kirk/O'Neill
37. Harley/Travers/Carr/Campbell
38. McCarron/Jackson/Gallagher/McFadden/Rudd/Gormley
39. Frazer/Muldoon/Tierney/O'Kane
40. Boyle/McKinney/Green/Doherty
41. Thompson/Muldoon/McFadden/Moran/Doherty
42. McCarron/Wilson/McAuley/Campbell/Griffith
43. Morrison/McCarron/Barr/Bradley/McCann
44. Moore/McNulty/Doherty
45. McCallion/Gillen/Kirk/Bradley/Matthewson/Flynn
46. McDermott/Ferguson/Tierney/McKernan/Crossan/Bradley
47. Lamberton/O'Kane/Deane
48. Green/Ryan/Doherty
49. McCann/Brennan
50. Organ/Hegarty/McAuley
51. O'Kane/McCool/Rodgers/Graham
52. Devlin/McMenamin/Shiels/Gallagher/Herrick/McCarron/Deeney
53. Bonney/Doherty & Hume/Boyle
54. Downey/Clift/O'Neill/Ferguson/McGilloway
55. Hegarty/Cassidy/Boyle/Devine
56. Friel/Doherty/McFerran
57. Downey/Bell/Quinn
58. Dalton/Higgins/Rooney
59. Connor/Brogan
60. Maguire/McConnell

61. Meenan/Phillips
62. McMenamin/Collins
63. Keogh/Jackson/Maguire
64. Collins & Harris/Keogh/Melly
65. Doherty/Strain/Canning
66. McIntyre/Ferguson/Coyle/ Billington/McCay
67. Goode/Healy
68. McCay/Lynch/Kivelehan/Clift/ Boyce
69. McGowan/Moore/Meenan/Devine
70. Murphy/Bradley/Friel
71. Meenan/Tierney/O'Hagan
72. Doyle/Donnelly/Doherty/Dalzell/ Doherty
73. Harkin/Boyle/Ziff/Pritchard/ McCarthy
74. Moore
75. Kirk/Wallace/McSheffrey/ McShane

Rossville Flats Shops (Ground floor, facing Joseph Street/Place)
1. Elizabeth McCrudden/Coyle's chemist/butcher shop/wool shop
2. Molly & Brendan Barr's newsagents/Dorrian's newsagents
3. Andrew Sheerin's grocery/Quinn's chemist
4. Hugh Quigley's grocery
5. Robert & Eileen Brown's hairdressers/playschool
6. Kathleen Gallagher/Ann Loughrey/Anne & Joe Harley's chip shop/Tommy Ho's restaurant
7-9. Nora and William Doherty's bakery and grocery/Frank McCoy's chip shop, co-op and arcade
9a. David Allen advertisement stand

Faces from the Flats

Children at the Rossville Flats playschool.

Making the best of things and enjoying the craic. Includes Eddie Meenan, Tommy Wilson, Gary Meenan and Brian Bonner.

Rossville Rovers football team. Includes Freddie Keogh, Patsy McGowan, Patsy Pickett, Michael Ryan, Paul McGuinness, Dick Tucker and Christopher McKnight.

Rossville Rovers. At back: Martin Dunleavy (manager) Paddy Slevin, Paul Chambers, Danny Wade, Gary Masterson, Sean Collins and Paddy Brennan. Front: Brian Dunleavy, Jim Phelan, Martin Dunleavy, Barry Wade, Mickey McFadden, Joe Cunningham and William Wilson.

A Rossville Rovers select with guests.

Above: Includes Gary Meenan, Sammy Kineton, Charles O'Neill,
Terry Meenan, Joe Cunningham, Eddie Meenan, Gareth Pritchard,
Seamus McConnell and Charles Lamberton.
Below: Includes Charles Lamberton, Charles O'Neill, Joe Cunningham,
Terry Meenan, Gareth Pritchard, Gary Meenan, Seamus McConnell,
Sammy Kineton, Paul Kineton and Eddie Meenan.

Just messing around: Liam Duffy, Conal McCourt, Darren Wilson, Edward Devine,
Kevin Quigley and Paul Devine.

Bridie O'Brien (née O'Reilly) and baby.

Sammy Rodden,
Terry Meenan,
Georgie Kineton
and Charles
Lamberton
examine a bullet
hole in the side
of the flats.

Paddy McGrellis and Kiera Coyle.

Emmett Tierney and Saoirse Ó Comáin.

Eugene Coyle, Charles (Porky) O'Neill, John McDevitt, Georgie Doherty, John White, Charlie (Chas) Gormley, Jim (Tubby) Friel, Kieran Pritchard, Terry Lamberton and Jim Collins.

Ellen Hutton, Gerard Coyle, Nichola and Shauna Quigg.

Peter Hutton and friend.

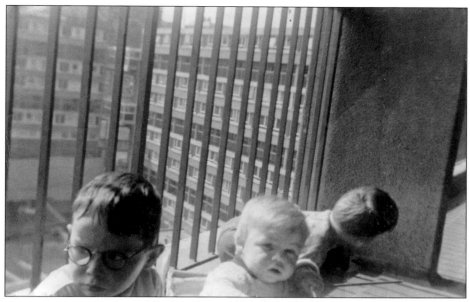

Charles, Gary and Mickey O'Neill.

Bridie Bonner relaxing with
Marie Coyle (née Hutton).

Brian Gallagher with Gerry and Liam
McGarrigle.

Rose, Dick,
Christy, Pat and
Derek Tucker.

Children's birthday party in the Fergusons' flat.

Gerald Coyle with son Gerald.

Marguerite and Sean Ryan with Gretta McConomy and friends.

Kathleen Hutton and family.

Gerald Coyle and Shauna Quigg are all smiles with the new baby.

Liam McGarrigle with Gerry and Tony Strain.

Margaret Quigg and daughter.

Edel Rankin and Mickey O'Neill on the stairway of the flats.

Eddie Collins, Fergal McDaid, Kieran Pritchard and Liam Brogan.

Frankie O'Neill, Melissa Ryan, Valerie McDaid, Annette Harkin (née Ryan), Trevor Lamberton and Elaine Ryan.

Leo, Jim, Joe, Billy (Bap), Mary and Jean Friel with James Barr and Mickey Coyle.

Young members of the Dunleavy family.

Liam and Adrian
McGarrigle.

Paul and Pat Strain with Gerry McGarrigle.

Gerald Coyle, Donna Hutton, Shauna
Quigg and Sally O'Neill.

Jim Collins with children
Elaine and Tracey.

Sharron, William, John, Catherine and Tommy Wilson.

Children at the Rossville Flats playschool.

Julie Dunlop, Cathy Laird (née Ryan), Corrina
Lamberton and Elaine Ryan.

Gerry McGarrigle and Donna
Swarth.

Paul, Philomena and Clarissa McLaughlin.

Elaine Logue (née McDevitt) with
Willie and Gary Meenan.

Joe, Jim and John Friel.

Shauna and Nicola Quigg.

Philly Wilson and Nancy Meenan.

Mrs Hutton and grandchild.

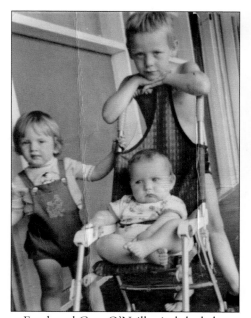

Frank and Gary O'Neill mind the baby.

Harry and Delia Bonney with their
children Dhana, Siobhan and Michelle.

Kieran Pritchard, Charles (Tweet) Lamberton, Dee's Doherty, Gareth (Screw) Pritchard
and Georgie Doherty.

Terry, Georgie, Kitty and Jimmy Kirk.

Rosie Tucker.

Eileen Collins with her family Jim, Patrick, Elaine and Tracey.

Paul Strain.

Emmett Tierney, John Ferguson, John Tierney and Sean Ferguson.

Gerald Coyle.

Hugh Dalzell with Áine.

Mary and Brian Tierney with baby Lynne.

Enjoying a summer break away. Includes Gary O'Neill, Trevor Lamberton,
John Tierney, Marie Doherty, Catherine McGowan, Michael Kelly,
Gary Johnston, Michael McFadden and Aaron Villa.

Commemorating the first anniversary of Bloody Sunday in 1973.